Selling is Warfare

Whether you are a sales person, a sales manager, or a business owner, you can profit from this new version of the world's most powerful guide to success. For over twenty-five hundred years, *The Art of War* has helped people like you succeed at competition.

In our sales version, *The Art of Sales,* we apply Sun Tzu's timeless principles to sales competition. *The Art of Sales* adapts Sun Tzu's ideas to lessons winning and keeping customers. No matter how successful you have been at selling, *The Art of War plus The Art of Sales* will inspire you, excite you, and give you new tools to win the daily battles of the marketplace.

The Book is only the beginning...

This book contains **the secret password keys** that allow you to access the Clearbridge Owners' Training Site (see **www.clearbridge.com** for information). This site contains over a thousand of pages of FREE training material to help you master Sun Tzu's techniques. You can download slide shows, study guides, eBooks, screen savers, posters, and more.

Buy the book today and study its ideas forever!

Sun Tzu's
The Art of War
Plus
The Art of Sales

孫
子
兵
法

To my wife, Rebecca,
who makes it all fun!

Sun Tzu's
The Art of War
Plus
The Art of Sales

By
Gary Gagliardi

Clearbridge Publishing

Published by
Clearbridge Publishing

FIRST EDITION, Third Printing
Copyright 1999, 2002 © Gary Gagliardi

Manufactured in the United States of America
Front Cover Art by Gary Gagliardi
Back Cover photograph by Rebecca Gagliardi

Library of Congress Control Number: 99-64138
ISBN 1-929194-01-3
Clearbridge Publishing's books may be purchased for business, for any promotional use, or for special sales. Please contact:

Clearbridge PUBLISHING
P.O. Box 33772, Shoreline, WA 98133
Phone: (206)-533-9357 Fax: (206)546-9756
www.clearbridge.com
info@clearbridge.com

CONTENTS

How to Use this Book

This is a different type of book on selling. It addresses sales strategy in its most critical form. It won't give you any tricks for overcoming objections or clever phrases for closing a sale. There are plenty of books that address those techniques. Instead, this book focuses on the long-term issues. It teaches the kind of thinking, planning and decision-making that it takes to have a successful career in selling.

In developing this book, we directly follow the advice of Sun Tzu in his famous book, *The Art of War*. Sun Tzu wrote about war over twenty-five hundred years ago, but his philosophy continues to gain popularity today. His strategic approach to competition works well in any struggle for success and especially well in the modern business world.

The Art of War offers a distinct, non-intuitive system for succeeding in competition. Its teaches that certain key factors influence the outcome of any competitive situation and that victory goes—not to the strongest or the most aggressive—but to the person who best understands the nature of competition, that is, the arts of war.

I can offer a personal testimony on the power of Sun Tzu's ideas. His lessons guided me through a successful career in sales and sales management into becoming a business owner.

I wrote the first version of *The Art of Sales* over ten years ago to train my software company's sales people. Following its introduction, our company became one of the fastest growing, privately held companies in America, twice appearing on the *Inc.* 500 list. When we sold that business, we retained the rights to *The Art of Sales* because we appreciated its role in our success. Since then, this single book has grown into a complete line of books addressing modern competitive problems, creating a new, fast-growing business.

This book gives you the complete text of *The Art of War* plus the line-by line sales adaptation, *The Art of Sales*. We suggest that you read both side-by-side so you can more clearly appreciate the deep competitive nature of selling. As you read, analyze your sales environment and *make notes* about how to apply Sun Tzu's suggestions to your current situation.

The book first addresses large-scale issues in selling that other books usually overlook. Do you understand the importance and challenges of a career in sales? Are you committed to it? Are you working for the right company and selling the right products? The topics are addressed in the beginning chapters of the text. You cannot be successful in sales unless you are the right person selling the right products for the right reason.

As you read deeper into the book, the text delves into a variety of specific situations and conditions. Because of this, we recommend that you review these later chapters randomly every few weeks or months. You will draw different lessons from them depending upon your situation when you read them. The word "strategy" comes from the Greek for "the thinking of a general." Learning strategy means teaching yourself to see your situations in a new way. This is the value of Sun Tzu.

The Art of Sales converts Sun Tzu's ideas from the military arena to the world of the salesperson as consistently as possible. We start by defining selling as a battle for the customer's mind. The nation for whom the army fights becomes the company for whom the sales person sells. Winning the battle means getting the order.

In Sun Tzu's view, the secret to warfare is not just winning battles. It is winning quickly and economically. We must keep what we have won. Victory alone is not enough. Sun Tzu teaches that true success is "making victory pay," that is, making victory profitable and rewarding. We must be wary of costly "victories" that don't lead to long-term success.

This concept of victory maps extremely well onto any intelligent view of sales. Our purpose just isn't to get orders; it is winning and keeping customers. It is winning sales quickly and effortlessly. We want to win in a way that leaves us ready for the next sale, not so burnt-out that we need a vacation.

In creating a sales adaptation of Sun Tzu, the biggest challenge is in defining who "the enemy" is. Sometimes the enemy is a competitor who is trying to win away our customers. More often, however, we are engaged in a contest of wills with our prospects, the people that we are trying to sell. This raises the question: Is the customer really "the enemy?"

Strangely enough, Sun Tzu's unique view of warfare makes this problem less difficult to resolve than it might seem at first. Sun Tzu saw the enemy as a partner in warfare. All competitors work with their enemy to make victory possible. *The Art of War* does not teach an aggressive or antagonistic view of competition, but rather a cooperative one. Indeed, Sun Tzu teaches us to avoid direct conflict if at all possible. We usually lose battles because we are too quick to fight. Instead, we work to set up situations in which conflict is unnecessary and the enemy naturally surrenders.

This interpretation reflects any salesperson's natural preoccupation with the customer and the customer's thinking. Only occasionally do Sun Tzu's ideas about the enemy apply to our direct competitors. As sales people, we must know what our competitors are doing, but only occasionally should we take action directed at our competitors. Customers, not competitors, determine our fate. To use this book successfully, you have to appreciate customers and competitors and the roles that they play in your success.

Sun Tzu's view of competition is knowledge-intensive. He sees victory going to the person who is the most knowledgeable. He even recognizes creativity as a special and important type of knowledge. Business innovation and continual improvement flow naturally from his philosophy. In Sun Tzu, there is no substitute for good information. Knowledge means having better information than anyone else, as sales people, knowing more about our area of business than any of our competitors know.

Reading and rereading this book is simply the first step in mastering the warrior's world of competitive philosophy. Sun Tzu's system is sophisticated and deep. Much of its sophistication is not readily apparent simply from reading the text. For in-depth study of Sun Tzu's methods, we have created *The Warrior Class*, our on-line training center. It contains hundred of slides, text lessons, and tests to help you master *The Art of War*. Access to the on-line site is FREE to anyone owning our books. See **www.clearbridge.com** for more information on how to access *The Warrior Class*.

If you prefer to get your information in the form of books, audio, or video, much of the information on our *Warrior Class* web site is available in other forms. The diagrams of Sun Tzu's system shown in the on-line slide shows are further explained in our *The Amazing Secrets of Sun Tzu* series which includes a book, audio, and video seminar. The lessons from the web site are published in book form in our book, *The Warrior Class*.

As your sales career moves forward and you want to apply Sun Tzu's competitive principles to other parts of your life, you may find our other books useful. This sales version of *The Art of War* is just one of many versions and adaptations offered by Clearbridge Publishing. Our goal is to have a version of Sun Tzu's book for every common form of competitive challenge that we face in modern life. A partial list is shown in the back of this book. We suggest you visit **www.clearbridge.com** for a complete list of our current titles.

Gary Gagliardi, 2002

PLANNING

This is war.
It is the most important skill in the nation.
It is the basis of life and death.
It is the philosophy of survival or destruction.
You must know it well.

Your skill comes from five factors.
Study these factors when you plan war.
You must insist on knowing the nature of:
1. Military philosophy,
2. The weather,
3. The ground,
4. The commander,
5. And military methods.

It starts with your military philosophy.
Command your people in a way that gives them a higher
shared purpose.
You can lead them to death.
You can lead them to life.
They must never fear danger or dishonesty.

SALES ANALYSIS

This is selling.
It is the most important skill in any business.
It can bring you fortune or poverty.
It is your path to success or failure.
You must study sales seriously.

Five factors determine your skill.
Consider these factors when you analyze a sale.
You must know:
1. Your sales philosophy,
2. Your attitude,
3. Your market,
4. Your leadership,
5. And your sales process.

Selling begins with your sales philosophy.
When you sell, you must always share your customers' goals.
You will share your customers' failures.
You will share your customers' successes.
With this philosophy, you need not fear or lie to customers.

Next, you have the weather.
It can be sunny or overcast.
It can be hot or cold.
It includes the timing of the seasons.

Next is the terrain.
It can be distant or near.
It can be difficult or easy.
It can be open or narrow.
It also determines your life or death.

Next is the commander.
He must be smart, trustworthy, caring, brave and strict.

Finally, you have your military methods.
They include the shape of your organization.
This comes from your management philosophy.
You must master their use.

All five of these factors are critical.
As a commander, you must pay attention to them.
Understanding them brings victory.
Ignoring them means defeat.

Next is your attitude.
You can be enthusiastic or negative.
You can be interested or indifferent to others.
Your attitude changes over time.

Next is your marketplace.
It can be spread out or be close by.
It can be complicated or simple.
Your prospects' minds can be open or closed.
Choosing the right market determines success or failure.

Next is your leadership.
You must be smart, honest, caring, brave, and disciplined.

Finally, you need the right sales process.
This process depends on the organization you are selling.
You must always control the sales process.
You must understand your customers well.

All five of these factors are critical.
You must continuously analyze them.
You must understand them to be successful.
Ignore them and you will fail.

You must learn through planning.
You must question the situation.

You must ask:
Which government has the right philosophy?
Which commander has the skill?
Which season and place has the advantage?
Which method of command works?
Which group of forces has the strength?
Which officers and men have the training?
Which rewards and punishments make sense?
This tells when you will win and when you will lose.
Some commanders perform this analysis.
If you use these commanders, you will win.
Keep them.
Some commanders ignore this analysis.
If you use these commanders, you will lose.
Get rid of them.

Plan an advantage by listening.
This makes you powerful.
Get assistance from the outside.
Know the situation.
Then planning can create advantages and controls power.

Analysis reveals what is important in the sale.
You need to ask many questions.

You must ask:
Does your company offer a good product?
Do you have the sales skills you need?
Do you know the right time to sell to the customer?
Which sales process is right for the customer?
Which issues are important to the customer?
Do you know more than the competition?
Which sales are going to make you money?
The answers tell which sales you win and which you lose.
You must act on this type of analysis.
If you use it, you will be successful.
You will have a good sales career.
Too many sales people ignore this analysis.
If you don't use it, your efforts will fail.
Your sales career will be short.

You discover your customers' interests by listening.
Listening gives you influence.
Listening makes it easy to win sales.
Listening is power.
Understand customers' desires and you can guide them.

Warfare is one thing.
It is a philosophy of deception.

When you are ready, you try to appear incapacitated.
When active, you pretend inactivity.
When you are close to the enemy, you appear distant.
When far away, pretend you are near.

If the enemy has strong position, entice him away from it.
If the enemy is confused, be decisive.
If the enemy is solid, prepare against him.
If the enemy is strong, avoid him.
If the enemy is angry, frustrate him.
If the enemy is weaker, make him arrogant.
If the enemy is relaxed, make him work.
If the enemy is united, break him apart.
Attack him when he is unprepared.
Leave when he least expects it.

You will find a place where you can win.
Don't pass it by.

Selling is one thing.
You must control your customers' perceptions.

If you have an advantage, you must seem humble.
If you are struggling, you must seem calm.
If you are convinced, you must seem uncertain.
When you are uncertain, you must appear confident.

If your customers are confident, entice them.
If your customers are confused, offer them leadership.
If your customers are successful, learn from them.
If some prospects don't need you, avoid them.
If your customers are easily excited, get them excited.
If your customers are insecure, build up their confidence.
If your customers are easygoing, save them effort.
If your customers are single-minded, wear them down.
Ask for the sale when they don't expect it.
Change your offer to surprise them.

You must find customers who need you.
Don't pass them by.

Before you go to war, you must believe that you can count
on victory.
You must calculate many advantages.
Before you go to battle, you may believe that you can foresee
defeat.
You can count few advantages.
Many advantages add up to victory.
Few advantages add up to defeat.
How can you know your advantages without analyzing them?
We can see where we are by means of our observations.
We can foresee our victory or defeat by planning.

Before closing a sale, you must know that the customer will buy your product.

The customer must have good reasons to buy.

Before wasting your time, you can see when you will not win the customer.

You can find too few reasons to buy.

Having good reasons to buy wins you customers.

Having too few reasons to buy wastes your time.

How can you prioritize actions without analyzing them?

You can see where you are only by means of questioning.

You can foresee winning the sale or losing it by analysis.

GOING TO WAR

Everything depends on your use of military philosophy.
Moving the army requires thousands of vehicles.
These vehicles must be loaded thousands of times.
The army must carry a huge supply of arms.
You need ten thousand acres of grain.
This results in internal and external shortages.
Any army consumes resources like an invader.
It uses up glue and paint for wood.
It requires armor for its vehicles.
People complain about the waste of a vast amount of metal.
It will set you back when you raise tens of thousands of troops.

Using a large army makes war very expensive to win.
Long delays create a dull army and sharp defeats.
Attacking enemy cities drains your forces.
Long campaigns that exhaust the nation's resources are wrong.

Choosing to Sell

Everything depends on your sales philosophy.
Traveling to see customers is expensive.
Building a territory takes time.
You want plenty of sales support from your company.
You want to be paid thousands of dollars in advances.
This results in a large investment from your company.
This drains resources from elsewhere in the company.
You want the best quality in sales resources.
You want others to support your efforts.
Others complain about how well sales people are paid.
You take your time selling when you can depend on
advances against future sales.

Selling slowly is too costly to be successful.
A complacent sales person always loses to a hungry one.
Long periods without a sale drain your enthusiasm.
Long sales cycles that deplete your company's resources
are wrong.

Manage a dull army.
You will suffer sharp defeats.
Drain your forces.
Your money will be used up.
Your rivals multiply as your army collapses and they will begin
against you.
It doesn't matter how smart you are.
You cannot get ahead by taking losses!

You hear of people going to war too quickly.
Still, you won't see a skilled war that lasts a long time.

You can fight a war for a long time or you can make your
nation strong.
You can't do both.

You can never totally understand all the dangers in using
arms.
Therefore, you can never totally understand the advantages in
using arms either.

You want to make good use of war.
Do not raise troops repeatedly.
Do not carry too many supplies.
Choose to be useful to your nation.
Feed off the enemy.
Make your army carry only the provisions it needs.

What happens when you are complacent?
You lose sales to someone who needs them more.
What happens when your enthusiasm fades?
You don't have the energy to continue.
As your sales efforts weaken, you inspire your competitors
to attack you.
It doesn't matter how smart you think you are.
You can't get ahead once you've fallen behind.

You can sometimes move too fast in a sales process.
However, the longer the sale cycle, the more often you fail.

You can try to play it safe when you sell or you can be
successful.
You can't have it both ways.

You can never completely insure against failure when you
sell.
You are therefore unlimited in the success that you can
achieve from sales.

You want to make good use of your efforts.
Do not repeatedly ask for new prospects or territory.
Do not continually request more resources.
Support the needs of your company.
Quickly earn business from your customers.
Limit yourself to the resources you truly need.

15

The nation impoverishes itself shipping to troops that are far
away.
Distant transportation is costly for hundreds of families.
Buying goods with the army nearby is also expensive.
These high prices also impoverish hundreds of families.
People quickly exhaust their resources supporting a military
force.
Military forces consume a nation's wealth entirely.
War leaves households in the former heart of the nation with
nothing.

War destroys hundreds of families.
Out of every ten families, war leaves only seven.
War empties the government's storehouses.
Broken armies will get rid of their horses.
They will throw down their armor, helmets, and arrows.
They will lose their swords and shields.
They will leave their wagons without oxen.
War will consume sixty percent of everything you have.

Because of this, the commander's duty is to feed off the
enemy.

Use a cup of the enemy's food.
It is worth twenty of your own.
Win a bushel of the enemy's feed.
It is worth twenty of your own.

You can kill the enemy and frustrate him as well.
Take the enemy's strength from him by stealing away his
supplies.

Selling into new prospects is costly for you and your company.
Trying to open new markets destroys many companies.
Conversely, selling into crowded markets is risky.
These high risks can also destroy your company.
When sales are slow, the company must accept orders of questionable value.
Lowering prices undermines your credibility entirely.
As a salesperson, cutting your prices to win a sale leaves you with nothing.

Many companies eventually fail.
Seven out of ten new businesses fail in two years.
The owners lose their investment.
Failed sales people must look for new employment.
You must give up the knowledge you've developed.
You may hope to find new uses for your ideas and abilities.
You have wasted your efforts to build a territory.
Six out of ten salespeople find other careers.

Because of this, you must generate your income from sales to existing prospects.

A dollar in commissions is worth twenty in salary or advances.
A dollar in customer sales today is worth twenty dollars of future potential.

Close sales aggressively.
You need to get the benefit of your customer's money as soon as possible.

Fight for the enemy's supply wagons.
Capture their supplies by using overwhelming force.
Reward the first who capture them.
Then change their banners and flags.
Mix them in with your own to increase your supply line.
Keep your soldiers strong by providing for them.
This is what it means to beat the enemy while you grow more
powerful.

Make victory in war pay for itself.
Avoid expensive, long campaigns.
The military commander's knowledge is the key.
It determines if the civilian officials can govern.
It determines if the nation's households are peaceful or a
danger to the state.

Fight for customers' business.
Win sales by offering your customers persuasive benefits.
Reward those who buy first.
Use these first customers to bring in more customers.
Base your presentation on customers' past success.
Their success is what makes you successful.
This is what it meant by helping the customer while helping yourself.

ᴓ—ᴊ

Make yourself successful by winning sales.
Don't make yourself poorer by lengthening sales cycles.
As a salesperson, your skill is the difference.
Good sales makes your product and company stronger.
Your sales skill determines how easy or difficult it is to sell your product.

💰

PLANNING AN ATTACK

Everyone relies on the arts of war.
A united nation is strong.
A divided nation is weak.
A united army is strong.
A divided army is weak.
A united force is strong.
A divided force is weak.
United men are strong.
Divided men are weak.
A united unit is strong.
A divided unit is weak.

Unity works because it enables you to win every battle you
fight.
Still, this is the foolish goal of a weak leader.
Avoid battle and make the enemy's men surrender.
This is the right goal for a superior leader.

Planning Your Territory

Everything depends on your selling skills.
A focused company is superior.
A diverse company is inferior.
A single product line is easy to sell.
Many different product lines are difficult to sell.
A concentrated effort is successful.
A divided effort fails.
A small territory is strong.
A spread-out territory is weak.
A unified message works well.
A mixed message works poorly.

You can meet a hundred objections and overcome them to win sales.
This doesn't make you a great salesperson.
You want to win sales without raising a single objection.
This is your highest goal.

The best policy is to attack while the enemy is still planning.
The next best is to disrupt alliances.
The next best is to attack the opposing army.
The worst is to attack the enemy's cities.

This is what happens when you attack a city.
You can attempt it, but you can't finish it.
First you must make siege engines.
You need the right equipment and machinery.
You use three months and still cannot win.
Then, you try to encircle the area.
You use three more months without making progress.
The commander still doesn't win and this angers him.
He then tries to swarm the city.
This kills a third of his officers and men.
He still isn't able to draw the enemy out of the city.
This attack is a disaster.

Make good use of war.
Make the enemy's troops surrender.
You can do this fighting only minor battles.
You can draw their men out of their cities.
You can do it with small attacks.
You can destroy the men of a nation.
You must keep your campaign short.

It's best to sell before the prospect starts shopping.
The next best is to sell though referrals.
The next best is to show better value than the alternatives.
The worst is to attack a customer's past decisions.

What happens when you try to change customers' minds?
You create resistance that works against you.
First, you must prepare arguments against their decisions.
You need to find leverage to change their thinking.
This can take months.
You must be persistent enough to turn them around.
After months of talking, most prospects will still not agree.
When you can't get agreement, you become frustrated.
You try to pressure customers into agreement.
You waste your limited time trying to persuade them.
The result is that you fail to win sales.
This type of selling is a disaster.

Make good use of your time.
You can win new customers.
You can do it without a single disagreement.
You can win customers away from their current suppliers.
You don't have to attack their past decisions directly.
You must focus your efforts on avoiding resistance.
You must find ways to win customers quickly.

You must use total war, fighting with everything you have.
Never stop fighting when at war.
You can gain complete advantage.
To do this, you must plan your strategy of attack.

The rules for making war are:
If you outnumber the enemy ten to one, surround them.
If you outnumber them five to one, attack them.
If you outnumber them two to one, divide them.
If you are equal, then find an advantageous battle.
If you are fewer, defend against them.
If you are much weaker, evade them.

Small forces are not powerful.
However, large forces cannot catch them.

You must master command.
The nation must support you.

Supporting the military makes the nation powerful.
Not supporting the military makes the nation weak.

Politicians create problems for the military in three different
ways.
Ignorant of the army's inability to advance, they order an
advance.
Ignorant of the army's inability to withdraw, they order a
withdrawal.
We call this tying up the army.
Politicians don't understand the army's business.
Still, they think they can run an army.
This confuses the army's officers.

24

In sales, you commit everything to winning customers.
Never stop selling when you are with prospects.
You can gain the advantage if you focus.
To do this, you must plan your sales strategy.

The rules for winning customers are:
If your product is ten times better, just take orders.
If your product is five times better, assume the sale.
If your product is twice as good, pick better prospects.
If your product is equal, sell only to the best prospects.
If your product is weaker, sell where competition cannot.
If your product is much weaker, find market niches.

Small companies cannot sell broad markets.
However, large companies cannot satisfy niche markets.

As a sales person, you control your territory.
Your territory must support you.

You are strong when your territory is well managed.
Your position is weak when the territory is poorly managed.

Poor territory management creates problems for sales
people in three ways.
Ignorant of which prospects are good, you try to sell to
everyone.
Ignorant of which prospects are bad, you are discouraged
from selling anyone.
You tie yourself up in knots.
Ignorant of management, you want different prospects.
You think you are in the wrong market.
This undermines the effectiveness of your efforts.

Politicians don't know the army's chain of command.
They give the army too much freedom.
This will create distrust among the army's officers.

The entire army becomes confused and distrusting.
This invites the invasion from many different rivals.
We say correctly that disorder in an army kills victory.

You must know five things to win:
Victory comes from knowing when to attack and when to
avoid battle.
Victory comes from correctly using large and small forces.
Victory comes from everyone sharing the same goals.
Victory comes from finding opportunities in problems.
Victory comes from having a capable commander and the
government leaving him alone.
You must know these five things.
You then know the theory of victory.

We say:
"Know yourself and know your enemy.
You will be safe in every battle.
You may know yourself but not know the enemy.
You will then lose one battle for every one you win.
You may not know yourself or the enemy.
You will then lose every battle."

You must understand your priorities in selling.
You cannot sell whoever and whenever you feel like it.
This creates weak customer relationships.

You confuse your prospects and create distrust.
This invites the competition to win away your customers.
A disorganized territory destroys your chances of success.

You must know five things to win customers.
You must know which prospects to sell and which
prospects to avoid.
You must know when to sell big and when to sell small.
You must know how to share your customers' goals.
You must know how to turn problems into opportunities.
You must know when to work your customers and when to
leave them alone.
Master these five categories of knowledge.
You then know the philosophy of winning sales.

Pay attention.
Know your products and your prospects.
If you do, you can win sales in any situation.
You may know your products, but not your prospects.
Then, for every sale you make, you will lose another.
You may know neither your products nor your prospects.
Then, you will lose every sale.

POSITIONING

Learn from the history of successful battles.
Your first actions should deny victory to the enemy.
You pay attention to your enemy to find the way to win.
You alone can deny victory to the enemy.
Only your enemy can allow you to win.

You must fight well.
You can prevent the enemy's victory.
You cannot win unless the enemy enables your victory.

We say:
You see the opportunity for victory; you don't create it.

You are sometimes unable to win.
You must then defend.
You will eventually be able to win.
You must then attack.
Defend when you have insufficient strength to win.
Attack when you have more strength than you need to win.

SALES POSITION

Learn from your past successes.
Never waste time on prospects you cannot sell.
Find prospects that you can win.
Only you can create the situation where the sale is lost.
Only the customer can make the purchase.

You must develop relationships.
You can prevent the loss of a sale.
You cannot force the customer to buy.

Pay attention:
You must see the opportunity to close; you can't create it.

You are not always positioned to win a sale.
Therefore, you must keep the sales process going.
You will eventually be in position to win the sale.
Then you must ask for the order.
Stay in the sale when you are not in a position to close it.
Close the sale when you are certain you will win it.

You must defend yourself well.
Save your forces and dig in.
You must attack well.
Move your forces when you have a clear advantage.

You must protect your forces until you can completely
triumph.

Some may see how to win.
However, they cannot position their forces where they must.
This demonstrates limited ability.

Some can struggle to a victory and the whole world may
praise their winning.
This also demonstrates a limited ability.

Win as easily as picking up a fallen hair.
Don't use all of your forces.
See the time to move.
Don't try to find something clever.
Hear the clap of thunder.
Don't try to hear something subtle.

Learn from the history of successful battles.
Victory goes to those who make winning easy.
A good battle is one that you will obviously win.
It doesn't take intelligence to win a reputation.
It doesn't take courage to achieve success.

You must nurture the sale carefully.
Say little and learn about the customer's business.
You must close sales decisively.
Demand customer action when the benfits are clear.

Keep yourself in contention for the sale until you are
certain to win it.

8—🔑

You may see what customers need.
Yet you fail to convince them that you meet those needs.
This shows a limited ability.

You may win a difficult sale that requires a great deal of
effort.
This also shows a limited ability.

Good sales are effortless.
Avoid using all your resources.
Vision is seeing what is obvious.
Don't try to find something hidden.
Hearing the customer is easy if you listen.
Don't imagine what you want to hear.

Learn from your successful efforts.
Winning sales requires making the job easy.
A good sale is one that you simply assume you will win.
You are foolish if you want to make a name for yourself.
Avoid conflict if you want to have real success in selling.

31

You must win your battles without effort.
Avoid difficult struggles.
Fight when your position must win.
You always win by preventing your defeat.

You must engage only in winning battles.
Position yourself where you cannot lose.
Never waste an opportunity to defeat your enemy.

You win a war by first assuring yourself of victory.
Only afterward do you look for a fight.
Outmaneuver the enemy before the battle and then fight to
win.

You must make good use of war.
Study military philosophy and the art of defense.
You can control your victory or defeat.

. This is the art of war.
1. Discuss the distances.
2. Discuss your numbers.
3. Discuss your calculations.
4. Discuss your decisions.
5. Discuss victory.
The ground determines the distance.
The distance determines your numbers.
Your numbers determine your calculations.
Your calculations determine your decisions.
Your decisions determine your victory.

You want to win sales without fighting your prospects.
Avoid sales battles.
Close sales when you are certain you will win.
Sell to customers who have already sold themselves.

You must sell only to customers that you can win.
Position yourself where you cannot lose the sale.
Await your opportunity and then ask for the order.

You must first know that the prospect needs your product.
Only then do you ask the prospect to decide.
You must never demand a decision to see what a prospect wants.

⚷

You must make good use of your time.
Examine your situation objectively.
Your discipline determines your success or failure.

The sales process requires:
1. A discussion of customer qualifications,
2. A discussion of customer needs,
3. A discussion of product value,
4. A discussion of your proposal,
5. And a discussion finalizing the sale.
Customers determine their qualifications.
Their qualifications determine their needs.
Their needs determine the value of the product.
Product value determines your proposal.
Your proposal determines how the sale is finalized.

Creating a winning war is like balancing a coin of gold against
a coin of silver.
Creating a losing war is like balancing a coin of silver against
a coin of gold.

Winning a battle is always a matter of people.
You pour them into battle like a flood of water pouring into a
deep gorge.
This is a matter of positioning.

You win sales when customers know that they are getting more than they give.
You will lose sales if they feel that they are giving more than they get.

You must be completely confident when you close a sale. The weight of benefits to the customer must be obvious and overwhelming.
This is the matter of your sales position.

MOMENTUM

You control a large army as you control a few men.
You just divide their ranks correctly.
You fight a large army the same as you fight a small one.
You only need the right position and communication.
You may meet a large enemy army.
You must be able to encounter the enemy without being defeated.
You must correctly use both surprise and direct action.
Your army's position must increase your strength.
Troops flanking an enemy can smash them like eggs.
You must correctly use both strength and weakness.

It is the same in all battles.
You use a direct approach to engage the enemy.
You use surprise to win.

You must use surprise for a successful invasion.
Surprise is as infinite as the weather and land.
Surprise is as inexhaustible as the flow of a river.

PERSUASION

Complex sales are the same as simple ones.
You only need to divide your time among more people.
Sales to large companies are the same as sales to small ones.
You need to understand their organization.
You may meet larger competitors.
You can compete against them and you should never lose a sale to them.
You only need to use creative and standard methods.
Together, they increase your influence with a prospect.
You must attack the competition on their weakness.
You must understand both their strengths and weaknesses.

In selling, you must use standard approaches in making contact with a prospect.
Your creativity wins the sale.

You must use creativity to be successful in all sales.
Creativity uses the unique conditions of the situation.
No sale is ever exactly the same.

You can be stopped and yet recover the initiative.
You must use your days and months correctly.

If you are defeated, you can recover.
You must use the four seasons correctly.

There are only a few notes in the scale.
Yet, you can always rearrange them.
You can never hear every song of victory.

There are only a few basic colors.
Yet, you can always mix them.
You can never see all the shades of victory.

There are only a few flavors.
Yet, you can always blend them.
You can never taste all the flavors of victory.

You fight with momentum.
There are only a few types of surprises and direct actions.
Yet, you can always vary the ones you use.
There is no limit in the ways you can win.

Surprise and direct action give birth to each other.
They proceed from each other in an endless cycle.
You can not exhaust all their possible combinations!

If you are creative, you can be rejected and yet return.
Yesterday's failure becomes tomorrow's new approach.

If you are creative, you can lose a sale and still recover.
You can lose one season and come back the next.

There are only a few basic sales techniques.
Yet, you can combine them any number of ways.
You can always find a better way to sell.

There are only a few basic human needs.
Yet, every person feels them differently.
You must always find your prospect's unique perspective.

There are only a few kinds of value.
Yet, it changes from person to person, moment to moment.
You can discover new benefits from customers.
.
You win sales with persuasion.
You only use a few creative and standard techniques.
Yet you can combine them to make each process unique.
You have no limit to the ways you can win.

Creative and standard approaches require each other.
You must use both and move from one to the other.
If you use both, no one can stop you.

Surging water flows together rapidly.
Its pressure washes away boulders.
This is momentum.

A hawk suddenly strikes a bird.
Its contact alone kills the prey.
This is timing.

You must fight only winning battles.
Your momentum must be overwhelming.
Your timing must be exact.

Your momentum is like the tension of a bent crossbow.
Your timing is like the pulling of a trigger.

War is complicated and confused.
Battle is chaotic.
Nevertheless, you must not allow chaos.

War is sloppy and messy.
Positions turn around.
Nevertheless, you must never be defeated.

Chaos gives birth to control.
Fear gives birth to courage.
Weakness gives birth to strength.

You must control chaos.
This depends on your planning.
Your men must brave their fears.
This depends on their momentum.

Creativity gives impact to ideas.
The force of your ideas can wash away resistance.
This is persuasion.

You close the sale with good timing.
Asking for the order at the right time overcomes resistance.
This is closing.

Success in sales depends on your skill.
Your creativity must be persuasive.
You must time your closing exactly.

Persuasion should increase the tension in the sale.
Closing should release that tension in a moment.

Sales are always complicated and confused.
Selling is messy.
It is your job to put order into the process.

Your position in the sale is never clear.
It is constantly changing.
Nevertheless, you must never lose the sale.

Your customer's confusion requires your clarity.
Your customer's uncertainty requires your confidence.
Your customer's weakness requires your strength.

You must clarify what is confused.
This depends on your analysis.
You must overcome uncertainty.
This depends on your persuasiveness.

You have strengths and weaknesses.
These come from your position.

You must force the enemy to move to your advantage.
Use your position.
The enemy must follow you.
Surrender a position.
The enemy must take it.
You can offer an advantage to move him.
You can use your men to move him.
You use your strength to hold him.

You want a successful battle.
To do this, you must seek momentum.
Do not just demand a good fight from your people.
You must pick good people and then give them momentum.

You must create momentum.
You create it with your men during battle.
This is comparable to rolling trees and stones.
Trees and stones roll because of their shape and weight.
Offer men safety and they will stay calm.
Endanger them and they will act.
Give them a place and they will hold.
Round them up and they will march.

You make your men powerful in battle with momentum.
This is just like rolling round stones down over a high, steep
cliff.
Use your momentum.

You have both strengths and weaknesses.
They arise from your position.

You must always take the lead in moving the sale forward.
Offer different types of proposals.
Your customers must think about them.
Offer customers something without risk.
They will want to take it.
You can use promotional offers to move them.
You can use your ideas to motivate them.
You can use your certainty to prevent a bad decision.

You must create the perfect situation for closing the sale.
You work toward it by building your influence.
You do not demand the sale from the customer.
You offer a great proposal and then you use real persuasion.

You must keep the sale moving forward.
You do this by keeping the prospect engaged.
One task must naturally lead to another.
The process must keep them moving.
Satisfaction with the status quo keeps them from acting.
Problems force them to act.
Solid information gets their attention.
Surround customers with information and they must act.

You make yourself powerful in a sale with persuasion.
You want everything moving inevitably toward a decision
in your favor.
Use persuasion.

WEAKNESS AND STRENGTH

Always arrive first to the empty battlefield to await the
enemy at your leisure.
If you are late and hurry to the battlefield, fighting is more
difficult.

You want a successful battle.
Move your men, but not into opposing forces.

You can make the enemy come to you.
Offer him an advantage.
You can make the enemy avoid coming to you.
Threaten him with danger.

When the enemy is fresh, you can tire him.
When he is well fed, you can starve him.
When he is relaxed, you can move him.

DISADVANTAGES AND ADVANTAGES

You want the advantage of getting to the customer before the competition does.
Avoid selling to prospects where the competition is already entrenched.

Your only goal is to win sales.
Use your time; don't waste it on the competition.

You can make customers come to you.
You must entice them with unique benefits.
You can stop the competition from attacking you.
Make it clear that they are wasting their time.

If prospects are comfortable, make them uncomfortable.
If prospects are satisfied, make them hungry for more.
If prospects are lethargic, ask them to do something.

Leave any place without haste.
Hurry to where you are unexpected.
You can easily march hundreds of miles without tiring.
To do so, travel through areas that are deserted.
You must take whatever you attack.
Attack when there is no defense.
You must have walls to defend.
Defend where it is impossible to attack.

Be skilled in attacking.
Give the enemy no idea of where to defend.

Be skillful in your defense.
Give the enemy no idea of where to attack.

Be subtle! Be subtle!
Arrive without any clear formation.
Quietly! Quietly!
Arrive without a sound.
You must use all your skill to control the enemy's decisions.

Advance where they can't defend.
Charge through their openings.
Withdraw where the enemy cannot chase you.
Move quickly so that they cannot catch you.

Abandon an established position slowly.
Quickly stake out markets before the competition does.
You can make easy progress in any sale.
To do so, you must uncover unexplored possibilities.
You must be certain to close every sale you go after.
You do this by only going after prospects who need you.
You must always keep customers that you have won.
You must leave no needs for your competition to satisfy.

You must be skilled in winning customers.
Fill needs that the competition overlooks.

You must be skilled in keeping customers.
Leave no unmet needs for the competition to exploit.

You must be clever about your intentions.
Don't let the customer assume they know what you offer.
You must be secretive about your proposals.
Don't let competitors know with whom you are working.
You must use your skill to control customers' thinking.

Make sales progress where customers can't resist you.
Attack the areas where they need help.
Quickly withdraw any ideas that create a conflict.
Change your position so the customer can't fight you.

I always pick my own battles.
The enemy can hide behind high walls and deep trenches.
I do not try to win by fighting him directly.
Instead, I attack a place that he must rescue.
I avoid the battles that I don't want.
I can divide the ground and yet defend it.
I don't give the enemy anything to win.
Divert him from coming to where you defend.

I make their men take a position while I take none.
I then focus my forces where the enemy divides his forces.
Where I focus, I unite my forces.
When the enemy divides, he creates many small groups.
I want my large group to attack one of his small ones.
Then I have many men where the enemy has but a few.
My large force can overwhelm his small one.
I then go on to the next small enemy group.
I will take them one at a time.

We must keep the place that we've chosen as a battleground
a secret.
The enemy must not know.
Force the enemy to prepare his defense in many places.
I want the enemy to defend many places.
Then I can choose where to fight.
His forces will be weak there.

You must pick your sales situations.
Customers can be secretive and protective.
You must not propose your product directly.
Instead, discover customers' goals and address them.
You must avoid sales conflicts.
You can defend your customers from any competitor.
Don't leave the competition any needs to satisfy.
Divert competitors from coming after your accounts.

ठ—ᴦ

Learn customers' positions and keep yourself flexible.
Identify a few key areas where customers have needs.
When you focus, you become more powerful.
When customers divide their attention, they create needs.
You must focus all your attention on their needs.
Spend your time where customers have not spent theirs.
You use your knowledge to overcome their lack of it.
You must offer one small idea at a time to help them.
You must lead them one step at a time.

ठ—ᴦ

You must keep your prospects, plans, and proposals a
secret.
You competition must not know them.
Force them to defend against every possible argument.
They will spread themselves too thin.
You can choose the key issues to fight them on.
They are unable to prepare in those areas.

If he reinforces his front lines, he depletes his rear.
If he reinforces his rear, he depletes his front.
If he reinforces his right, he depletes his left.
If he reinforces his left, he depletes his right.
Without knowing the place of attack, he cannot prepare.
Without a place, he will be weak everywhere.

The enemy has weak points.
Prepare your men against them.
He has strong points.
Make his men prepare themselves against you.

You must know the battle ground.
You must know the time of battle.
You can then travel a thousand miles and still win the battle.

The enemy should not know the battleground.
He shouldn't know the time of battle.
His left will be unable to support his right.
His right will be unable to support his left.
His front lines will be unable to support his rear.
His rear will be unable to support his front.
His support is distant even if it is only ten miles away.
What unknown place can be close?

We control the balance of forces.
The enemy may have many men but they are superfluous.
How can they help him to victory?

If they focus on price, they hurt their claims of best quality.
If they focus on quality, they hurt their claims of low prices.
If they focus on quickness, they weaken claims of accuracy.
If they focus on accuracy, they weaken claims of quickness.
Without knowing your issue, they cannot fight you directly.
If they claim every advantage, they are weak everywhere.

Customers have needs.
You must prepare to address them.
The competition has strengths.
Make them try to attack you on your strengths.

You must know the customer's key issues.
You must know when the customer needs to buy.
You can then win the sale despite strong competition.

Your competition may not know the key issues.
They should never know when you are asking for the sale.
Let them sell inappropriate ideas as well as good ones.
The inappropriate ones discredit their good ideas.
Let them sell useless features as well as valuable ones.
The useless features raise the cost of their valuable ones.
You can let them claim that they have a good product.
They can still miss the customer's needs.

You can influence the sense of value in the sale.
Your competitor can have too many features.
Are they valuable if the customer doesn't need them?

We say:
You must let victory happen.

The enemy may have many men.
You can still control him without a fight.

When you form your strategy, know the strengths and
weaknesses of your plan.
When you execute, know how to manage both action and
inaction.
When you take a position, know the deadly and the winning
grounds.
When you battle, know when you have too many or too few
men.

Use your position as your war's centerpiece.
Arrive at the battle without a formation.
Don't take a position.
Then even the best spies can't report it.
Even the wisest general cannot plan to counter you.
Take a position where you can triumph using superior
numbers.
Keep the enemy's forces ignorant.
Their troops will learn of my location when my position will
win.
They must not know how our location gives us a winning
position.
Make the battle one from which they cannot recover.
You must always adjust your position to their position.

Pay attention:
You must let yourself win the sale.

The competition may have a much bigger company.
You can still control them without a direct battle.

When you plan, know your customers' strengths and weaknesses.
In meetings, know when to persuade and when you need to listen.
When you take a position, know what is important to customers and what isn't.
When you sell, know if you addressing too many or too few of their needs.

The best policy for any salesperson is to remain flexible.
Don't go into a sale with a standard product offering.
Avoid initial proposals.
Then the competition cannot discredit your proposal.
You can beat them if they don't know what to expect.
Take a position when you see an opportunity to use your influence.
Keep your competition in the dark.
Their sales people may learn about your proposal when it will win.
They should never know why your proposal is so pleasing to the customer.
Make sure your proposal is one that they cannot counter.
You must adapt proposals to the key issues of the customer.

Manage your military position like water.
Water takes every shape.
It avoids the high and moves to the low.
Your war can take any shape.
It must avoid the strong and strike the weak.
Water follows the shape of the land that directs its flow.
Your forces follow the enemy who determines how you win.

Make war without a standard approach.
Water has no consistent shape.
If you follow the enemy's shifts and changes, you can always
win.
We call this shadowing.

Fight five different campaigns without a firm rule for victory.
Use all four seasons without a consistent position.
Your timing must be sudden.
A few weeks determine your failure or success.

You must remain flexible in the sales process.
Like water, you can take any shape.
Water naturally moves from the high and flows to the low.
You can adjust to any situation.
You must avoid strength and attack weakness.
Water follows the shape of the land that directs its flow.
You follow your customers' needs to create your offer.

You must avoid a rigid sales presentation.
Water has no consistent shape.
You win sales by following customers and adapting to their needs.
Act on their signals.

Use different tactics; no single approach always wins.
No specific time and no single proposal are always right.
You must always create a sense of urgency.
An instant may determine your success or failure.

Armed Conflict

Everyone uses the arts of war.
You accept orders from the government.
Then you assemble your army.
You organize your men and build camps.
You must avoid disasters from armed conflict.

Seeking armed conflict can be disastrous.
Because of this, a detour can be the shortest path.
Because of this, problems can become opportunities.

Use an indirect route as your highway.
Use the search for advantage to guide you.
When you fall behind, you must catch up.
When you get ahead, you must wait.
You must know the detour that most directly accomplishes
your plan.

Undertake armed conflict when you have an advantage.
Seeking armed conflict for its own sake is dangerous.

SALES CONTACT

Everyone uses the art of sales.
You accept your assignment from the company.
You assemble your leads and prospects.
You happily organize and build them into a territory.
However, the most difficult job is sales contact.

Sales contact is uncomfortable for everyone.
You cannot plan the path it will take.
You must expect problems and turn them into opportunities.

You must plan to take an indirect route to your goal.
You must plan to entice customers with benefits.
When you stumble, you must know how to catch up.
When you get ahead of the customer, you must slow down.
You must know how to plan for both objections and
acceptance.

You alone can make the sales contact successful.
All customer contact is inherently difficult.

You can build up an army to fight for an advantage.
Then you won't catch the enemy.
You can force your army to go fight for an advantage.
Then you abandon your heavy supply wagons.

You keep only your armor and hurry straight after the enemy.
You avoid stopping day or night.
You use many roads at the same time.
You go hundreds of miles to fight for an advantage.
Then the enemy catches your commanders and your army.
Your strong soldiers get there first.
Your weaker soldiers follow behind.
Using this approach, only one in ten will arrive.
You can try to go fifty miles to fight for an advantage.
Then your commanders and army will stumble.
Using this method, only half of your soldiers will make it.
You can try to go thirty miles to fight for an advantage.
Then only two out of three get there.

If you make your army travel without good supply lines, they
will die.
Without supplies and food, your army will die.
If you don't save the harvest, your army will die.

Do not let any of your potential enemies know of what you
are planning.

You can offer many arguments about product benefits.
You will then lose the customer.
You can rush through the sales process proposing benefits.
You then fail to learn about the customer.

You can defend your product and ask directly for the order.
You can work day and night.
You can work with many different customer contacts.
You can spend all your time preaching product benefits.
The customer can still reject your product and company.
You think you are winning the sale at first.
Over time your weaknesses will show.
Only a small fraction of your effort is useful.
You can try smaller shortcuts in the sales process.
Your proposals will still fall short.
You are wasting half of your time.
You can rush sales that are almost complete.
You may win two out of three.

You can try to shortcut a sales process, but it will cost you sales.
Without the proper information, you lose sales.
Without the proper groundwork, you lose sales.

Instead, you must initially keep quiet about what you are planning to sell.

Still, you must not hesitate to form alliances.
You must know the lay of the land.
You must know where the obstructions are.
You must know where the marshes are.
If you don't, you cannot move the army.
You must use local guides.
If you don't, you can't take advantage of the terrain.

You make war using a deceptive position.
If you use deception, then you can move.
Using deception, you can upset the enemy and change the situation.
You must move as quickly as the wind.
You must rise like the forest.
You must invade and plunder like fire.
You must stay as motionless as a mountain.
You must be as mysterious as the fog.
You must strike like sounding thunder.

Divide your troops to plunder the villages.
When on open ground, dividing is an advantage.
Don't worry about organization, just move.
Be the first to find a new route that leads directly to a winning plan.
This is the how you are successful at armed conflict.

You must meet with people and talk with them.
You must know the customer's business.
You must know where their problems are.
You must avoid bogging down in politics.
You must be knowledgeable to make the sale.
You must rely on your contacts in the business.
You must take advantage of the customer's thinking.

You must disguise your desire to make a sale.
If the customer doesn't fight you, you can make progress.
You uncover their problems, understand them, and use the situation
To make sales, you must think on your feet.
You must eventually stand up and make your point.
You must be aggressive and hungry.
You must be quiet and patient.
You must keep your plans to yourself.
You must be bold and courageous.

When managing your territory, prioritize your activities.
When an opportunity offers itself, come to an agreement.
Don't think about it, just act.
Find better ways to help customers find success in their businesses.
This is the how you are successful at customer contact.

Military experience says:
"You can speak, but you will not be heard.
You must use gongs and drums.
You cannot really see your forces just by looking.
You must use banners and flags."

You must master gongs, drums, banners and flags.
Place people as a single unit where they can all see and hear.
You must unite them as one.
Then, the brave cannot advance alone.
The fearful cannot withdraw alone.
You must force them to act as a group.

In night battles, you must use numerous fires and drums.
In day battles, you must use many banners and flags.
You must position your people to control what they see and
hear.

You control your army by controlling its emotions.
As a general, you must be able to control emotions.

In the morning, a person's energy is high.
During the day, it fades.
By evening, a person's thoughts turn to home.
You must use your troops wisely.
Avoid the enemy's high spirits.
Strike when they are lazy and want to go home.
This is how you master energy.

Experience in sales teaches us:
"Words alone are not enough.
Use pictures and charts.
Demonstrating is not enough.
Use showmanship and magic."

Use pictures, props, and showmanship to get everyone's
attention.
Tie your arguments together.
Don't offer innovative ideas alone.
Tie them with comfortable, familiar ideas.
Every idea must amplify a single, clear message.

When unknown, you must create excitement and interest.
If you are better known, you still must keep it interesting.
You must take a position that everyone can understand and
appreciate.

⚷

You must get your customers' attention.
As a salesperson, you must use emotion.

In the morning, customer resistance is high.
During the day, it fades.
By evening, they want to go home.
You must use your time wisely.
Avoid tough resistance.
Close when resistance fades and they want to go home.
This is how you master energy.

Use discipline to await the chaos of battle.
Keep relaxed to await a crisis.
This is how you master emotion.

Stay close to home to await a distant enemy.
Stay comfortable to await the weary enemy.
Stay well fed to await the hungry enemy.
This is how you master power.

Don't entice the enemy when their ranks are orderly.
You must not attack when their formations are solid
This is how you master adaptation.
You must follow these military rules.
Do not take a position facing the high ground.
Do not oppose those with their backs to wall.
Do not follow those who pretend to flee.
Do not attack the enemy's strongest men.
Do not swallow the enemy's bait.
Do not block an army that is heading home.
Leave an escape outlet for a surrounded army.
Do not press a desperate foe.
This is the art of war.

Keep organized when the customer is confused.
Stay quiet while the customer blows off steam.
This is how you master your feelings.

Stick to your point and wait for others to respond.
Stay friendly as you wear down the customer's resistance.
You will be successful if you serve the needs of others.
This is how you master persuasion.

Do not create organized resistance.
Do not attack firmly held beliefs.
This is how you master adapting.
You must follow these sales rules.
Do not take a position against strong feelings.
Do not fight an argument based on a lack of alternatives.
Do not accept those who only pretend to agree.
Do not attack the strongest competition against you.
Do not believe everything the customer tells you.
Do not argue with a customer who agrees with you.
Give the customer an agreeable alternative.
Do not press the customer too hard for a decision.
These are the rules of selling.

ADAPTABILITY

Everyone uses the arts of war.
As a general, you get your orders from the government.
You gather your troops.
On dangerous ground, you must not camp.
Where the roads intersect, you must join your allies.
When an area is cut off, you must not delay in it.
When you are surrounded, you must scheme.
In a life-of-death situation, you must fight.
There are roads that you must not take.
There are armies that you must not fight.
There are strongholds that you must not attack.
There are positions that you must not defend.
There are government commands that must not be obeyed.

Military leaders must be experts in knowing how to adapt to
win.
This will teach you the use of war.

ADJUSTING TO THE SITUATION

There are basic rules in selling.
You get your territory from the company.
You organize your sales process.
When the sale is impossible, you must not waste your time.
When you share goals, you must make partners.
When you are rejected, you must not give up.
When you are outmaneuvered, you must get creative.
When you are in a do-or-die situation, you must win.
There are products and services you should not sell.
There are customers that you don't want.
There are competitors that you cannot challenge.
There are proposals that you must not defend.
There are times when you ignore standard company policy.

You must become an expert at knowing how to adapt to win a sale.
Adapting to the situation is the key to success.

Some commanders are not good at making adjustments to
find an advantage.
They can know the shape of the terrain.
Still, they can not find an advantageous position.

Some military commanders do not know how to adjust their
methods.
They can find an advantageous position.
Still, they can not use their men effectively.

You must be creative in your planning.
You must adapt to your opportunities and weaknesses.
You can use a variety of approaches and still have a
consistent result.
You must adjust to a variety of problems and consistently
solve them.

You can deter your potential enemy by using his weaknesses
against him.
You can keep your enemy's army busy by giving it work to do.
You can rush your enemy by offering him an advantageous
position.

Some sales people are unable to change their positions to fit a given situation.
They might know what the customer thinks.
Still, they are unable to identify the key issues in the sale.

Some sales people attempt to sell without changing their usual methods.
They can figure out what the key issues are.
Still, they are unable to adjust so they can address them.

♉︎━☇

You must be inventive in planning the sale.
You can find strengths and weaknesses in every situation.
You can use different approaches and still consistently win sales.
Every situation offers unique problems, but you can always find a good solution.

♉︎━☇

You can overcome competitors by using their weaknesses against them.
You must force your competitors to defend their products.
You can speed the sales process by giving customers a good reason to decide now.

♉︎━☇

You must make use of war.
Do not trust that the enemy isn't coming.
Trust on your readiness to meet him.
Do not trust that the enemy won't attack.
We must rely only on our ability to pick a place that the
enemy can't attack.

You can exploit five different faults in a leader.
If he is willing to die, you can kill him.
If he wants to survive, you can capture him.
He may have a quick temper.
You can then provoke him with insults.
If he has a delicate sense of honor, you can disgrace him.
If he loves his people, you can create problems for him.
In every situation, look for these five weaknesses.
They are common faults in commanders.
They always lead to military disaster.

To overturn an army, you must kill its general.
To do this, you must use these five weaknesses.
You must always look for them.

You must use your resources carefully.
Do not expect to win any sale without resistance.
Instead, be ready to meet resistance.
Do not trust that competitors won't attack your product.
Instead, position your product so that others can't easily
attack it.

Salespeople can have five different character flaws.
If they are willing to lose a sale, they will lose it.
If they lack courage, they will give products away.
If they have a quick temper, you can provoke them.
If they are sensitive to rejection, they can't ask for an order.
If they are sensitive to criticism, you can embarrass them.
If they love their arguments, they will get into trouble.
In every situation, look for these five weaknesses.
They are common faults in salespeople.
They can lead you to disaster in sales.

These weaknesses can destroy you and your career.
You must know how to exploit them in others.
You must always be aware of them.

ARMED MARCH

Everyone moving their army must adjust to the enemy.

Keep out of the mountains and in the valleys.
Position yourself on the heights facing the sun.
To win your battles, never attack uphill.
This is how you position your army in the mountains.

When water blocks you, keep far away from it.
Let the enemy cross the river and wait for him.
Do not meet him in midstream.
Wait for him to get half his forces across and then take
advantage of the situation.

You need to be able to fight.
You can't do that if you are in the water when you meet an
attack.
Position yourself upstream, facing the sun.
Never face against the current.
Always position your army upstream when near the water.

Moving Sales Forward

To move the sales forward, adjust to the customer.

Within large organizations, start low in the organization.
Work up to management and getter better known.
To win the sale, never fight upper management.
This is how you work within large hierarchies.

In companies with many divisions, respect their boundaries
Wait until your competitor crosses departmental lines.
Don't copy them in ignoring boundaries.
When they start trying to sell to your contacts, you can
easily beat them.

You must stay competitive.
Don't depend on divisional boundaries to stop the
competition.
Move decisions higher up in the organization.
Make the competition battle the politics of the company.
Always work above them in the organization.

You may have to move across marshes.
Move through them quickly without stopping.
You may meet the enemy in the middle of a marsh.
You must keep on the water grasses.
Keep your back to a clump of trees.
This is how you position your army in a marsh.

On a level plateau, take a position that you can change.
Keep the higher ground on your right and to the rear.
Keep the danger in front of you and safety behind.
This is how you position yourself on a level plateau.

You can find an advantage in all four of these situations.
Learn from the great emperor who used positioning to
conquer his four rivals.

Armies are stronger on high ground and weaker on low.
They are better camping on sunny, southern hillsides than on
the shady, northern ones.
Provide for your army's health and place it well.
Your army will be free from disease.
Done correctly, this means victory.

You must sometimes defend on a hill or riverbank.
You must keep on the south side in the sun.
Keep the uphill slope at your right rear.

This will give the advantage to your army.
It will always give you a position of strength.

Complex organizations can bog you down.
Move quickly through them to find the real decision maker.
You can encounter competition in confusing organizations.
When you do, try to establish a well defined sales process.
You don't want the competition to surprise you.
You must avoid missteps in these companies.

In a flat organization, offer flexible proposals.
Move as high as you can to promote your product.
Watch the competition and keep your champions safe.
Champions win sales within flat organizations.

You can win sales in all four types of organizations.
Successful sales people use the organization to beat their
competition.

§—⚔

The higher within an organization, the stronger you are.
Introduce yourself to the top people as readily as the lower
ones.
Healthy relationships come from your value to people.
You must keep your relationships productive.
Do this correctly and you will win customers.

Sometimes you must defend a slight advantage.
Make the value of your product known to the top people.
You always want the top people behind you.

These relationships can only benefit your efforts.
It gives you a position of strength.

§—⚔

Stop the march when the rain swells the river into rapids.
You may want to ford the river.
Wait until it subsides.

All regions have dead-ends such as waterfalls.
There are deep lakes.
There are high cliffs.
There are dense jungles.
There are thick quagmires.
There are steep crevasses.
Get away from all these quickly.
Do not get close to them.
Keep them at a distance.
Maneuver the enemy close to them.
Position yourself facing these dangers.
Push the enemy back into them.

Danger can hide on your army's flank.
There are reservoirs and lakes.
There are reeds and thickets.
There are forests of trees.
Their dense vegetation provides a hiding place.
You must cautiously search through them.
They can always hide an ambush.

Stop selling during a change in organizational structure.
You can still win the sale.
Wait until company changes resolve themselves.

All organizations have barriers.
There are nay-sayers.
There are gatekeepers.
There are time-wasters.
There are deal-killers.
There are lawyers.
Get past them quickly.
Do not invest your time in them.
Keep them at a distance.
Put your competition in touch with them.
Keep your eye on these people.
Let your competitors be blind-sided by them.

Opposition can be hidden.
Beware of committees.
Beware of task forces.
Beware of bureaucracies.
They can provide a secret base for competitive attack.
You must carefully search through them.
You don't want them to ambush you.

Sometimes, the enemy is close by but remains calm.
Expect to find him in a natural stronghold.
Other times, he remains at a distance but provokes battle.
He wants you to attack him.

He sometimes shifts the position of his camp.
He is looking for an advantageous position.

The trees in the forest move.
Expect that the enemy is coming.
The tall grasses obstruct your view.
Be suspicious.

The birds take flight.
Expect that the enemy is hiding.
Animals startle.
Expect an ambush.

Notice the dust.
It sometimes rises high in a straight line.
Vehicles are coming.
The dust appears low in a wide band.
Foot soldiers are coming.
The dust seems scattered in different areas.
The enemy is collecting firewood.
Any dust is light and settling down.
The enemy is setting up camp.

Competition is involved in the sale but they are quiet.
You should expect that they have a safe position.
The competition says little about you but pursues the sale.
They want you to attack their product.

Competitors may make their proposal easy to attack.
Always expect that they have a secret advantage.

The goals of the purchase may suddenly change.
This means that the competition has been active.
There are too many purchasing requirements.
Suspect the competition is creating them.

Your contacts may suddenly become shy.
Suspect that the competition is planning a surprise.
Your supporters may become uncertain.
The competitor is ambushing you.

Listen for rumors about the competition.
News about competition can come from top managers.
This means that the competition is aggressive.
You hear about the competition from everywhere.
This means they have many people in the account.
News of the competition is scattered in different areas.
This means that they are learning about the organization.
News of the competition becomes rarer and rarer.
This means that they are inactive.

Your enemy speaks humbly while building up forces.
He is planning to advance.

The enemy talks aggressively and pushes as if to advance.
He is planning to retreat.

Small vehicles exit his camp first and move to positions on
the army's flanks.
They are forming a battle line.

Your enemy tries to sue for peace but without offering a
treaty.
He is plotting.

Your enemy's men run to leave and yet form ranks.
You should expect action.

Half his army advances and the other half retreats.
He is luring you.

Your enemy plans to fight but his men just stand there.
They are starving.

Those who draw water drink it first.
They are thirsty.

Your enemy sees an advantage but does not advance.
His men are tired.

Birds gather.
Your enemy has abandoned his camp.

Your competitors seem pessimistic but active.
Expect them to increase pressure.

Your competitors claim victory and attack you.
Expect them to give up soon

Your competitors ask a prospect for a number of small decisions.
Expect them to try to close the sale.

Your competitors offer to give you the sale without anything in return.
Expect them to try to trick you.

Your competitors start actively organizing.
Expect them to call for a decision.

Your competitors offer to split the sale with you.
This means that they are laying a trap.

Your competitors start offering discounts in price.
This means that they aren't making sales.

Your competitors start asking for cash payments.
They are out of money.

Your competitors have a clear opportunity but do nothing.
This means that they are lazy.

Customers start coming to you.
This means that your competitor has abandoned them.

Your enemy's soldiers call in the night.
They are afraid.

Your enemy's army is raucous.
They do not take their commander seriously.

Your enemy's banners and flags shift.
Order is breaking down.

Your enemy's officers are irritable.
They are exhausted.

Your enemy's men kill their horses for meat.
They are out of provisions.

They don't put their pots away or return to their tents.
They expect to fight to the death.

Enemy troops appear sincere and agreeable.
But their men are slow to speak to each other.
They are no longer united.

Your enemy offers too many incentives to his men.
He is in trouble.

Your enemy gives out too many punishments.
His men are weary.

Your enemy first attacks and then is afraid of your larger
force.
His best troops have not arrived.

Competitors ask you for information.
This means that they are afraid.

The competition's claims are dismissed.
This means that they are not taken seriously.

The competition's sales proposals suddenly change.
This means that they are disorganized.

The competition's management is restless.
This means that their salespeople are ineffective.

Your competitors let their customers dictate terms.
This means that they are out of resources.

Competitors offer desperate proposals.
Expect them to fight you to the end.

The competition seems sincere and dedicated.
Nevertheless, they speak poorly of their management.
This means that they are not dedicated to their company.

The competition offers too many incentives to buy.
This means that they are in trouble.

Your competitor starts giving customers time limits.
This means that they are under pressure.

Your competitors first attack you and then try making
friends with you.
This means that they are not too bright.

Your enemy comes in a conciliatory manner.
He needs to rest and recuperate.

Your enemy is angry and appears to welcome battle.
This goes on for a long time, but he doesn't attack.
He also doesn't leave the field.
You must watch him carefully.

If you are too weak to fight, you must find more men.
In this situation, you must not act aggressively.
You must unite your forces, expect the enemy, recruit men
and wait.

You must be cautious about making plans and adjust to the
enemy.
You must increase the size of your forces.

With new, undedicated soldiers, you can depend on them if
you discipline them.
They will tend to disobey your orders.
If they do not obey your orders, they will be useless.

You can depend on seasoned, dedicated soldiers.
But you must avoid disciplining them without reason.
Otherwise, you cannot use them.

You must control your soldiers with *esprit de corp*.
You must bring them together by winning victories.
You must get them to believe in you.

Competitors try to collaborate with you.
This means that they need your help.

Competitors sell aggressively but do not close the sale.
They are in the sale for a long time, but never attack you.
They never give up the sale either.
In these situations, you must be cautious.

If your position cannot win the sale, you can build it up.
However, you must not ask the customer for the order.
You must focus your efforts, prepare for the competition,
and bide your time.

You must plan continuously and never take your
competitors lightly.
You must never let the competition get ahead of you.

You must take a firm position in new customer
relationships.
Otherwise, they will not accept your leadership.
If they do not see your leadership, you have no control.

It is different with established customer relationships.
You must show flexibility.
They serve you best by giving you new ideas.

You must establish strong customer relationships.
You must win customers by making them successful.
They must believe in you.

Make it easy for them to obey your orders by training your
people.
Your people will then obey you.
If you do not make it easy to obey, you won't train your
people.
Then they will not obey.

Make your commands easy to follow.
You must understand the way a crowd thinks.

Make it easy for customers to buy from you by educating them.
They will then order from you repeatedly.
If you make it difficult to buy, you won't keep your customers.
They will stop listening to you.

You must make it easy to buy.
You must always educate your customers.

FIELD POSITION

Some field positions are unobstructed.
Some field positions are entangling.
Some field positions are supporting.
Some field positions are constricted.
Some field positions give you a barricade.
Some field positions are spread out.

You can attack from some positions easily.
Others can attack you easily as well.
We call these unobstructed positions.
These positions are open.
On them, be the first to occupy a high, sunny area.
Put yourself where you can defend your supply routes.
Then you will have an advantage.

CUSTOMER RELATIONSHIPS

Some customers are accessible.
Some customers are exclusive.
Some customers are supportive.
Some customers are narrow-minded.
Some customers are one-man shows.
Some customers are unqualified.

Notice when customers freely accept you.
They will accept the competition as easily.
These are accessible customers.
These customers are open to new ideas.
With these customers, be the first to understand their needs.
Work with their top people and position products clearly.
With them, leadership is essential.

You can attack from some positions easily.
Disaster arises when you try to return to them.
These are entangling positions.
These field positions are one-sided.
Wait until your enemy is unprepared.
You can then attack from these positions and win.
Avoid a well prepared enemy.
You will try to attack and lose.
Since you can't return, you will meet disaster.
These field positions offer no advantage.

I cannot leave some positions without losing an advantage.
If the enemy leaves this ground, he also loses an advantage.
We call these supporting field positions.
These positions strengthen you.
The enemy may try to entice me away.
Still, I will hold my position.
You must entice the enemy to leave.
You then strike him as he is leaving.
These field positions offer an advantage.

Some field positions are constricted.
I try to get to these positions before the enemy does.
You must fill these areas and await the enemy.
Sometimes, the enemy will reach them first.
If he fills them, do not follow him.
But if he fails to fill them, you can go after him.

Some customers give you one shot at getting their business.
You cannot go back to them after striking out.
These are exclusive customers.
They give you one chance.
Wait and identify an issue that requires your help.
You can then go after them and win their business.
Avoid selling to them if you don't solve a real problem.
Your attempts will fail.
Since you can't come back, you waste your only chance.
You cannot control these customers.

Some customers go with whomever is the most persistent.
Neither you nor your competition can give up on them
without losing.
These are supportive customers.
Know when a customer is supportive..
You must stay with them.
If competition seems to give up, stay with the customer.
You must convince the competition to lose their patience.
You want this type of customer.

Some customers are narrow-minded.
You must contact these customers first.
You must influence them and then wait for the competition.
The competition may contact them first.
If they win over the decision maker, don't waste your time.
But if they fail to win them, you can go after them.

Some field positions give you a barricade.
I get to these positions before the enemy does.
You occupy their southern, sunny heights and wait for the
enemy.
Sometimes the enemy occupies these areas first.
If so, entice him away.
Never go after him.

Some field positions are too spread out.
Your force may seem equal to the enemy.
Still you will lose if you provoke a battle.
If you fight, you will not have any advantage.

These are the six types of field positions.
Each battleground has its own rules.
As a commander, you must know where to go.
You must examine each position closely.

Some armies can be outmaneuvered.
Some armies are too lax.
Some armies fall down.
Some armies fall apart.
Some armies are disorganized.
Some armies must retreat.

Know all six of these weaknesses.
They lead to losses on both good and bad ground.
They all arise from the army's commander.

Some customers are one-man shows.
You must contact the decision maker first.
You must contact the top person and then invite in the competition.
Sometimes the competition gets to the head person first.
If so, lure the decision-maker away from them.
Do not sell them if competitors have won the top person.

Some customers are unqualified.
It may seem like you can convince them to buy.
But you are wasting your time selling to them.
Even if you make a sale, you will never benefit from it.

These are the six types of customers.
Each customer type has its own rules.
You must know who your customers are.
You must never stop asking questions.

There are sales people that rush.
There are sales people that are too slow.
There are sales people that stumble.
There are sales people that fall apart.
There are sales people that are disorganized.
There are sales people that give up.

You must avoid these six weaknesses.
These problems don't arise from your nature.
They come from your actions.

One general can command a force equal to the enemy.
Still his enemy outflanks him.
This means that his army can be outmaneuvered.

Another can have strong soldiers, but weak officers.
This means that his army will be too lax.

Another has strong officers but weak soldiers.
This means that his army will fall down.

Another has sub-commanders that are angry and defiant.
They attack the enemy and fight their own battles.
As a commander, he cannot know the battlefield.
This means that his army will fall apart.

Another general is weak and easygoing.
He fails to make his orders clear.
His officers and men lack direction,
This shows in his military formations.
This means that his army will be disorganized.

Another general fails to predict the enemy.
He pits his small forces against larger ones.
He puts his weak forces against stronger ones.
He fails to pick his fights correctly.
This means that his army must retreat.

You must know all about these six weaknesses.
You must understand the philosophies that lead to defeat.
When a general arrives, you can know what he will do.
You must study each one carefully.

Your products may be equal to the competition.
Still, you let the competition outmaneuver you.
This means that you are in a rush.

Your ideas are good, but your process is weak.
You will be too slow.

Your process is strong but your ideas are weak.
You will stumble.

You can neglect your sales contacts.
The people in the account don't help you.
Then you fail to get to know the customer.
You will fall apart.

You can be lazy and sloppy.
Your proposal is unclear.
If your proposal is unclear, customers lack direction.
Your time is not well spent.
You are disorganized.

As a salesperson, you can fail to understand the customer.
You offer solutions for problems they don't have.
You compete on the wrong issues.
You fail to pick the right customers.
You must eventually give up.

You must understand all six faults.
In order to win sales, you must avoid these weaknesses.
You must understand your customers.
The customer helps you make the sale.

Y‌ou must control your field position.
It will always strengthen your army.

You must predict the enemy to overpower him and win.
You must analyze the obstacles, dangers, and distances.
This is the best way to command.

Understand your field position before you go to battle.
Then you will win.
You can fail to understand your field position and still fight.
Then you will lose.

You must provoke battle when you will certainly win.
It doesn't matter what you are ordered.
The government may order you not to fight.
Despite that, you must always fight when you will win.

Sometimes provoking a battle will lead to a loss.
The government may order you to fight.
Despite that, you must avoid battle when you will lose.

You must advance without desiring praise.
You must retreat without fearing shame.
The only correct move is to preserve your troops.
This is how you serve your country.
This is how you reward your nation.

You must guide the customer.
This always strengthens your position.

You must foresee how to discredit the buyer's alternatives.
You must see the buyer's difficulties, problems, and needs.
This is the best way to win sales.

You must understand these issues when you close the sale.
If you do, you will always win the sale.
You may not understand these issues and try to close sales.
But you will always fail.

You must close when you are certain to get the sale.
Don't try to time the sale to meet your company's needs.
There may be many reasons why the timing isn't ideal.
Still, you must always close when the opportunity is there.

When you will lose the sale, you must delay the decision.
Your boss may insist that you to try to close the sale.
Still, you must prevent the decision when you will lose.

You must never close because you need the commission.
You must close without worrying if you will be rejected.
You should worry only about preserving your advantages.
You must help the customer to serve your own company.
This is how you make yourself successful.

Think of your soldiers as little children.
You can make them follow you into a deep river.
Treat them as your beloved children.
You can lead them all to their deaths.

Some leaders are generous, but cannot use their men.
They love their men, but cannot command them.
Their men are unruly and disorganized.
These leaders create spoiled children.
Their soldiers are useless.

You may know what your soldiers will do in an attack.
You may not know if the enemy is vulnerable to attack.
You will then win only half the time.
You may know that the enemy is vulnerable to attack.
You may not know if your men are capable of attacking them.
You will still win only half the time.
You may know that the enemy is vulnerable to attack.
You may know that your men are ready to attack.
You may not know how to position yourself in the field for battle.
You will still win only half the time.

You must know how to make war.
You can then act without confusion.
You can attempt anything.

Treat your customers as your children.
They will follow you.
Treat them with care and attention.
They will stay with you forever.

If you care about customers, you must ask them to buy.
If you love them, you must demand that they act.
You must not leave them confused—without guidance.
You cannot help them if they don't listen.
Your support is useless.

You can know that you have good products.
But you must also know their value to customers.
If you don't, you have only done half of your job.
You can know how to satisfy customer needs.
But you must still convince customers that your products
are good.
If you don't, you have only done half of your job.
You can know customers' needs.
You can know how your products serve their needs.
But you must also know exactly what your customers are
thinking.
If you don't, you have done only half of your job.

You must truly understand selling.
You can then act with certainty.
You can sell anything.

We say:
Know the enemy and know yourself.
Your victory will be painless.
Know the weather and the field.
Your victory will be complete.

Pay attention:
Know your customers and your products.
Then sales are effortless.
Understand customers' thinking and their needs.
Then your success is assured.

TYPES OF TERRAIN

Use the art of war.
Know when the terrain will scatter you.
Know when the terrain will be easy.
Know when the terrain will be disputed.
Know when the terrain is open.
Know when the terrain is intersecting.
Know when the terrain is dangerous.
Know when the terrain is bad.
Know when the terrain is confined.
Know when the terrain is deadly.

Warring parties must sometimes fight inside their own
territory.
This is scattering terrain.

When you enter hostile territory, your penetration is shallow.
This is easy terrain.

Some terrain gives me an advantageous position.
However, it gives others an advantageous position as well.
This will be disputed terrain.

102

Sales Situations

Use your sales skills:
Know when your situation is tenuous.
Know when your situation is easy.
Know when your situation is contentious.
Know when your situation is open.
Know when your situation is shared.
Know when your situation is serious.
Know when your situation is bad.
Know when your situation is restricting.
Know when your situation is do-or-die.

All customers are initially uneasy and distrustful with a
new salesperson.
This is a tenuous situation.

The customer is open to a sales call.
This is an easy situation.

The customer shows some interest.
However, they show interest in competing products as well.
This is a contentious situation.

I can use some terrain to advance easily.
Others can advance along with us.
This is open terrain.

Everyone shares access to a given area.
The first one there can gather a larger group than anyone
else.
This is intersecting terrain.

You can penetrate deeply into hostile territory.
Then many hostile cities are behind you.
This is dangerous terrain.

There are mountain forests.
There are rugged hills.
There are marshes.
Everyone confronts these obstacles on a campaign.
They make bad terrain.

In some areas, the passage is narrow.
You are closed in as you enter and exit them.
In this type of area, a few people can attack our much larger
force.
This is confined terrain.

You can sometimes survive only if you fight quickly.
You will die if you delay.
This is deadly terrain.

You make easy progress in the sale.
The competition, however, can still come in at any time.
This is an open situation.

Complementary companies can work together on a sale.
The first one in the account can determine the priorities in
the sales process.
This is a shared situation.

You invest a great deal of time in a sale.
The closer you get to closing, the more the customer resists.
This is a serious situation.

Some customers can't pay.
Others can't decide.
You can't make some customers happy.
These are serious problems in any sale.
These are bad situations.

Getting into many sales is difficult.
Getting out of some sales, however, is impossible.
You must make commitments that limit what you can and
cannot do.
These are restricting situations.

Sometimes you can win only if you close immediately.
Your will lose the sale if the process continues.
These are do-or-die situations

To be successful, you control scattering terrain by not
fighting.
Control easy terrain by not stopping.
Control disputed terrain by not attacking.
Control open terrain by staying with the enemy's forces.
Control intersecting terrain by uniting with your allies.
Control dangerous terrain by plundering.
Control bad terrain by keeping on the move.
Control confined terrain by using surprise.
Control deadly terrain by fighting.

Go to any area that helps you in waging war.
You use it to cut off the enemy's contact between his front
and back lines.
Prevent his small parties from relying on his larger force.
Stop his strong divisions from rescuing his weak ones.
Prevent his officers from getting his men together.
Chase his soldiers apart to stop them from amassing.
Harass them to prevent their ranks from forming.

When joining battle gives you an advantage, you must do it.
When it isn't to your benefit, you must avoid it.

A daring soldier may ask:
"A large, organized enemy army and its general are coming.
What do I do to prepare for them?"

To be successful in tenuous situations, avoid creating any resistance.

In easy situations, don't stop.

In contentious situations, don't press for a decision.

In open situations, don't try to block the competition.

In shared situations, bring in your handpicked allies.

In serious situations, move confidently as fast as possible.

In bad situations, get out and find another customer.

In restricting situations, look for alternatives.

In do-or-die situations, demand the order.

Find any area where you can help the customer.

You must control the flow of information to the customer about the market.

Keep the competition from developing many supporters.

Keep your different competitors at odds with one another.

Prevent them from getting together against you.

Discredit their proposals before they can gain credibility.

Discredit their company if their proposal seems acceptable.

When you have the advantages, force a confrontation.

When you don't have the advantages, avoid confrontation.

You may ask:

"A large, well-organized competitor is coming into my sale. What do should I do?"

Tell him:
"First seize an area that the enemy must have.
Then they will pay attention to you.
Mastering speed is the essence of war.
Take advantage of a large enemy's inability to keep up.
Use a philosophy of avoiding difficult situations.
Attack the area where he doesn't expect you."

You must use the philosophy of an invader.
Invade deeply and then concentrate your forces.
This controls your men without oppressing them.

Get your supplies from the riches of the territory.
It is sufficient to supply your whole army.

Take care of your men and do not overtax them.
Your *esprit de corps* increases your momentum.
Keep your army moving and plan for surprises.
Make it difficult for the enemy to count your forces.
Position your men where there is no place to run.
They will then face death without fleeing.
They will find a way to survive.
Your officers and men will fight to their utmost.

Military officers that are completely committed lose their fear.
When they have nowhere to run, they must stand firm.
Deep in enemy territory, they are captives.
Since they cannot escape, they will fight.

Pay attention.
Raise issues that customers must address quickly.
You can then guide them.
Urgency is the essence of sales.
Take advantage of a large competitor's inability to keep up.
Act without hesitation.
Keep the discussion where the competition is unprepared.

Act like a guest when you go into the customer's business.
When you invest your time, you must focus your efforts.
You must help the customer's people: do not fight them.

You must get your support from the internal champions.
The customer's needs must fuel your sales efforts.

Build support for your product, but do not oversell it.
Make customers feel like a vital part of your company.
Keep the sales process moving and expect surprises.
Always give customers more value than they expect.
Put yourself in a position where you must make the sale.
You cannot just go onto the next prospect.
You must find a way to help them.
You must commit all of your skills to win.

When you commit yourself, you lose your fear of rejection.
When you must win, you can be firm with customers.
When you are dedicated to customers, you have no choice.
You have no choice but to do everything you can.

Commit your men completely.
Without being posted, they will be on guard.
Without being asked, they will get what is needed.
Without being forced, they will be dedicated.
Without being given orders, they can be trusted.

Stop them from guessing by removing all their doubts.
Stop them from dying by giving them no place to run.

Your officers may not be rich.
Nevertheless, they still desire plunder.
They may die young.
Nevertheless, they still want to live forever.

You must order the time of attack.
Officers and men may sit and weep until their lapels are wet.
When they stand up, tears may stream down their cheeks.
Put them in a position where they cannot run.
They will show the greatest courage under fire.

Make good use of war.
This demands instant reflexes.
You must develop these instant reflexes.
Act like an ordinary mountain snake.
Someone can strike at your head.
You can then attack with your tail
Someone can strike at your tail.
You can then attack with your head.
Someone can strike at your middle.
You can then attack with both your head and tail.

Totally commit yourself.
Without being warned, you must be on guard.
Without being asked, you must answer expected questions.
Without being forced, your must consider customer needs.
Without being told, you must take initiative.

Stop second-guessing yourself and stay well informed.
Stop losing sales by giving yourself no excuse for losing.

Your efforts may fail.
This isn't because you can't make them successful.
You have failed before.
It wasn't because you didn't want success.

You must decide when to close the sale.
You may feel shy and uncertain
When you must ask for the order, you may fear rejection.
Put yourself in a position where you must win the sale.
You will find the courage you need.

𝕆━▸

Make good use of your selling.
You must respond with practiced precision.
Your must prepare to instantly overcome objections.
You should be able to act on reflex.
They will question your products' quality.
Know how to prove they are the best value for the price.
They will attack your products' pricing.
Instantly show how their quality is worth the investment.
They can question you on any issue.
Immediately respond with value and quality.

A daring soldier asks:
"Can any army imitate these instant reflexes?"
We answer:
"It can."

To command and get the most of proud people, you must
study adversity.
People work together when they are in the same boat during a
storm.
In this situation, one rescues the other just as the right hand
helps the left.

Use adversity correctly.
Tether your horses and bury your wagon's wheels.
Still, you can't depend on this alone.
An organized force is braver than lone individuals.
This is the art of organization.
Put the tough and weak together.
You must also use the terrain.

Make good use of war.
Unite your men as one.
Never let them give up.

The commander must be a military professional.
This requires confidence and detachment.
You must maintain dignity and order.
You must control what your men see and hear.
They must follow you without knowing your plans.

You may question this.
Can you sell using such instant responses?
There is only one answer.
You must!

Customers fear that you will attempt to mislead or
overcharge them.
Yet, you must both work together to solve each other's
problems.
You can both help each other if you realize that you are
partners in business.

You must lead customers correctly.
You want them to feel the need for your product.
This isn't, however, enough.
Give them a balanced picture so you win their confidence.
This is the art of persuasion.
You must show both your strengths and weaknesses.
You must know what is important.

Use your time well.
Make your presentation simple and focused.
You must never give up.

☗━✦

You must dedicate yourself to being a salesperson.
This requires confidence and detachment.
You must maintain your authority and control.
You must inspire your customers' vision and ideas.
They must believe you know more than they do.

You can reinvent your men's roles.
You can change your plans.
You can use your men without their understanding.

You must shift your campgrounds.
You must take detours from the ordinary routes.
You must use your men without giving them your strategy.

A commander provides what his army needs now.
You must be willing to climb high and then kick away your
ladder.
You must be able to lead your men deeply into your enemy's
territory and then find a way to create the opportunity that
you need.

You must drive men like a flock of sheep.

You must drive them to march.
You must drive them to attack.
You must never let them know where you are headed.
You must unite them into a great army.
You must then drive them against all opposition.
This is the job of a true commander.

You must adapt to the different terrain.
You must adapt to find an advantage.
You must manage your people's affections.
You must study all these skills.

You must find new possibilities in customers' businesses.
You must invent new approaches.
You must try new ideas without the assurance of success.

You must offer different proposals for every customer.
You must offer something different from your competition.
The customer should never anticipate you.

You must provide exactly what is needed at the moment.
You must be willing to go out on a limb and take a risk
when selling.
You must get deeply involved in a customer's business to
find the problems that create the opportunities that you
need to make the sale.

You must inspire customers to act.

You must inspire them to throw away the old.
You must inspire them to try something new.
You must never let them know where you are headed.
You must focus your proposals on critical issues.
You must overcome all objections.
This is the job of a true salesperson.

You must adapt to every sales situation.
You must adjust your methods to win the sale.
You must control customers' emotions.
You must master all these skills.

Always use the philosophy of invasion.
Deep invasions concentrate your forces.
Shallow invasions scatter your forces.
When you leave your country and cross the border, you must take control.
This is always critical ground.
You can sometimes move in any direction.
This is always intersecting ground.
You can penetrate deeply into a territory.
This is always dangerous ground.
You penetrate only a little way.
This is always easy ground.
Your retreat is closed and the path ahead tight.
This is always confined ground.
There is sometimes no place to run.
This is always deadly ground.

To use scattering terrain correctly, we must inspire our men's devotion.
On easy terrain, we must keep in close communication.
On disputed terrain, we should try to hamper the enemy's progress.
On open terrain, we must carefully defend our chosen position.
On intersecting terrain, we must solidify our alliances.
On dangerous terrain, we must ensure our food supplies.
On bad terrain, we must keep advancing along the road.
On confined terrain, we must make block flow from our headquarters.
On deadly terrain, we must show what we can do by killing the enemy.

You must act like a guest in a prospect's business.
In long sales cycles, focus your efforts on a few key ideas.
In short sales cycles, work with many prospects at once.
When you commit yourself to a customer, you must offer leadership.
This is a critical moment.
You can go to different departments.
Look for allies who share your goals.
You eventually reach the end of the process.
Expect serious objections.
You won't see objections at the beginning of the sale.
This is always the easy part of the sale.
Then your choices become fewer and more difficult.
These are restricting situations.
You must eventually close the sale.
This is a do-or-die situation.

To succeed in tenuous situations, you must get customers excited.
In easy situations, you must meet often with customers.
In contentious situations, your must create obstacles for your competitors.
In open situations, you must defend your position and your proposal.
In shared situations, you must control your partners.
In serious situations, you must have plenty of resources.
In bad situations, you must go on to another customer.
In restricting situations, you must defend your bottom line with the top decision-makers.
In do-or-die situations, you must prove yourself by closing the sale.

Make your men feel like an army.
Surround them and they will defend themselves.
If they cannot avoid it, they will fight.
If they are under pressure, they will obey.

Do the right thing when you don't know your different
enemies' plans.
Don't attempt to meet them.

You don't know the local mountains, forests, hills and
marshes?
Then you cannot march the army.
You don't have local guides?
You won't get any of the benefits of the terrain.

There are many factors in war.
You may lack knowledge of any one of them.
If so, it is wrong to take a nation into war.

You must be able to dominate a nation at war.
Divide a big nation before they are able to gather a large
force.
Increase your enemy's fear.
Prevent his forces from getting together and organizing.

Do the right thing and don't try to compete for outside
alliances.
You won't have to fight for authority.
Trust only yourself and your own resources.
This increases the enemy's uncertainty.
You can force one of his allies to pull out.
His whole nation can fall.

Shape your presentations to the customer's beliefs.
If you pressure them, they will fight you.
When you make it easy, they will buy.
When they need you, they will follow your lead.

🔑

Do the right thing when you don't understand the
prospect's business.
Admit that you aren't prepared to sell to them.

You don't really understand the prospect's organization and
their needs?
Then you can't move the sale forward.
You don't have information from within the company?
You won't know anyone's goals or needs.

There is so much to know.
You don't want to miss anything.
Otherwise, you won't control the results in the sale.

You must control everything in the sale.
Attack real problems before customers develop their own
solutions to them.
Get customers worried about their business.
Answer their questions so that they can't form objections.

Do the right thing and don't look for business allies to help
with every sale.
You won't have to fight for control.
Trust only yourself and your own resources.
This increases your customers' dependence on you.
You can convince competitors' allies to abandon them.
Their whole sales effort may then fail.

119

Distribute plunder without worrying about agreements.
Halt without the government's command.
Attack with the whole strength of your army.
Use your army as if it was a single man.

Attack with skill.
Do not discuss it.
Attack when you have an advantage.
Do not talk about the dangers.
When you can launch your army into deadly ground, even if
it stumbles, it can still survive.
You can be weakened in a deadly battle and yet be stronger
afterward.

Even a large force can fall into misfortune.
If you fall behind, however, you can still turn defeat into
victory.
You must use the skills of war.
To survive, you must adapt to your enemy's purpose.
You must stay with him no matter where he goes.
It may take a thousand miles to kill the general.
If you correctly understand him, you can find the skill to do
it.

Manage your government correctly at the start of a war.
Close your borders and tear up passports.
Block the passage of envoys.
Encourage politicians at headquarters to stay out of it.
You must use any means to put an end to politics.
Your enemy's people will leave you an opening.
You must instantly invade through it.

Working alone, you don't divide the profits.
You can change your proposal without negotiating.
You can focus all your resources.
You can work with a single goal.

You win sales for business reasons.
Don't brag about it.
You are judged by number of sales you win.
Don't worry about the ones you lose.
You can get into bad situations and lose sales, but you can still survive.
You may temporarily lose ground, but you can also learn from your mistakes.

You can win many times and still get into bad situations.
If you fall behind, however, you can still turn defeat into success.
You need to develop a professional attitude.
To sell, you must adapt completely to the customer needs.
You must stay with the customer no matter where they go.
You can invest months of time to win them.
If you are skillful, you can completely understand their businesses.

Do the right things at the beginning of a sale.
Keep quiet and forget past proposals.
Don't try to negotiate.
Get to know the top decision makers.
These are the people you must influence.
The customer will eventually give you an opportunity.
You must grab it quickly.

Immediately seize a place that they love.
Do it quickly.
Trample any border to pursue the enemy.
Use your judgment about when to fight.

Doing the right thing at the start of war is like approaching a
woman.
Your enemy's men must open the door.
After that, you should act like a streaking rabbit.
The enemy will be unable to catch you.

Quickly focus on goals that customers desire.
Waste no time.
Don't be afraid of barriers while pursuing the sale.
Use your judgement about when to sell.

You should begin every sales situation by carefully playing hard to get.
The customer will eventually give you an opening.
After that, you should act quickly and unpredictably.
The competition will be unable to catch up with you.

ATTACKING WITH FIRE

There are five ways of attacking with fire.
The first is burning troops.
The second is burning supplies.
The third is burning supply transport.
The fourth is burning storehouses.
The fifth is burning camps.

To make fire, you must have the resources.
To build a fire, you must prepare the raw materials.

To attack with fire, you must be in the right season.
To start a fire, you must have the time.

Choose the right season.
The weather must be very dry.

Choose the right time.
Pick a season when the grass is as high as the side of a cart.

You can tell the proper days by the stars in the night sky.
You want days when the wind rises in the morning.

Using Desire

There are five categories of customer desires:
The first is personal needs.
The second is the need for products.
The third is the need for information.
The fourth is the need for profit.
The fifth is the need for people.

To create desire, a product must have value to a customer.
To stimulate desire, you must know the customer's mind.

To sell using that desire, customers must feel their needs.
To close using desire, you must pick the right moment.

There is a right time to close the sale.
It is when customers' needs are at their peak.

Choose the right time to close sales.
Pick a time when customers have plenty of money.

To know the right time, read the customers' signals.
You want to pick a time that gives you influence.

Everyone attacks with fire.
You must create five different situations with fire and be able
to adjust to them.

You start a fire inside the enemy's camp.
Then attack the enemy's periphery.

You launch a fire attack, but the enemy remains calm.
Wait and do not attack.

The fire reaches its height.
Follow its path if you can.
If you can't follow it, stay where you are.

Spreading fires on the outside of camp can kill.
You can't always get fire inside the enemy's camp.
Take your time in spreading it.

Set the fire when the wind is at your back.
Don't attack into the wind.
Daytime winds last a long time.
Night winds fade quickly.

Every army must know how to deal with the five attacks by
fire.
Use many men to guard against them.

Everyone tries to address customer needs.
You must respond to the five types of needs and adjust to them.

You may address a central need of the company.
Then you can then deal with peripheral issues.

You uncover a problem that doesn't worry the customer.
Wait until they worry before you sell.
.
Some customers' needs demand attention now.
Present solutions immediately if you can.
If you can't address these issues, wait for a better time.

Publicizing needs can win sales.
In many situations, you can't get to the decision-maker.
Take your time promoting your solution.

You can fan customer desires.
Don't fight against prevailing attitudes.
Well-known needs get attention.
Subtle needs are easily overlooked.

You must master these five methods to harness customer desires.
Your sales process must prepare you to use them.

When you use fire to assist your attacks, you are being
clever.
Water can add force to an attack.
You can also use water to disrupt an enemy.
It doesn't, however, take his resources.

You win in battle by getting the opportunity to attack.
It is dangerous if you fail to study how to accomplish this
achievement.
As commander, you cannot waste your opportunities.

We say:
A wise leader plans success.
A good general studies it.
If there is little to be gained, don't act.
If there is little to win, do not use your men.
If there is no danger, don't fight.

As leader, you cannot let your anger interfere with the success
of your forces.
As commander, you cannot fight simply because you are
enraged.
Join the battle only when it is in your advantage to act.
If there is no advantage in joining a battle, stay put.

Anger can change back into happiness.
Rage can change back into joy.
A nation once destroyed cannot be brought back to life.
Dead men do not return to the living.

Leveraging customer desires to generate your sales is smart selling.
Persuasion can help you sell.
You can use persuasion to involve customers.
Persuasion alone, however, doesn't address the real issues.

You win customers by selling your strengths.
Additionally, you must carefully nurture your relationships with them.
In sales, you cannot afford to waste your efforts.

Pay attention!
If you are clever, you plan to win customers.
If you are truly clever, you plan to keep them.
If a customer has no long-term value, don't sell to them.
If the customer can't buy, don't waste your time.
If customers have no problems, don't sell to them.

You must never let your need for a money affect how you deal with a prospect.
You must never try to close a sale because your ego needs a victory.
Sell only when it is in your long-term advantage to sell.
If there is no benefit in selling, find another prospect.

Greed can change to poverty.
Pride can be easily humbled.
If you waste your time, you will not get it back.
Worthless customers cannot make you successful.

This fact must make a wise leader cautious.
A good general is on guard.

Your philosophy must be to keep the nation peaceful and the army intact.

Knowing this, you must be selective.
You must always be on watch for the best opportunities.

Your plan must be to pick the right customers and you build your territory.

USING SPIES

Altogether, building an army requires thousands of men.
They invade and march thousands of miles.
Whole families are destroyed.
Other families must be heavily taxed.
Every day, thousands of dollars must be spent.

Internal and external events force people to move.
They are unable to work while on the road.
They are unable to find and hold a useful job.
This affects seventy percent of thousands of families.

You can watch and guard for years.
Then a single battle can determine victory in a day.
Despite this, bureaucrats hold onto their salary money too
dearly.
They remain ignorant of the enemy's condition.
The result is cruel.

They are not leaders of men.
They are not servants of the state.
They are not masters of victory.

Using Questions

Becoming a successful sales person requires effort.
You have to travel thousands of miles.
You waste months of time.
Someone must pay for your efforts.
Every day, it costs money.

When selling, customer contact moves the process forward.
You waste your time if you are not talking to customers.
You can't always make progress in a sale.
Still, tremendous resources are required to support you.

You can work on a sale for years.
Then it can be decided in a single day.
Despite this, many sales people are too selfish with their time.
You cannot afford to stay ignorant about the customer.
Thinking you don't have the time to learn is foolishness.

Without information, you cannot guide the sale.
You are no help to your company.
You cannot win sales.

You need a creative leader and a worthy commander.
You must move your troops to the right places to beat others.
You must accomplish your attack and escape unharmed.
This requires foreknowledge.
You can obtain foreknowledge.
You can't get it from demons or spirits.
You can't see it from professional experience.
You can't check it with analysis.
You can only get it from other people.
You must always know the enemy's situation.

You must use five types of spies.
You need local spies.
You need inside spies.
You need double agents.
You need doomed spies.
You need surviving spies.

You need all five types of spies.
No one must discover your methods.
You will be then able to put together a true picture.
This is the commander's most valuable resource.

You need local spies.
Get them by hiring people from the countryside.

You need inside spies.
Win them by subverting government officials.

You need double agents.
Discover enemy agents and convert them.

You must be an intelligent, valuable leader.
You must spend time on the right issues to win any sale.
You must win your sales in a minimum of time.
This requires information.
You can get this information.
You won't get it from psychology.
You won't get it from past experience.
You can't reason it out.
You can only get it by asking questions of people.
You must always learn the customer's issues.

There are only five types of questions.
There are qualifying questions.
There are identifying questions.
There are value questions.
There are leading questions.
There are closing questions.

You must use all five types of questions.
If you do, no one will ever challenge your knowledge.
You can learn about any business and its workings.
This information is your most valuable resource.

You must ask qualifying questions.
Ask everyone about the basic condition of the business.

You must ask identifying questions.
Discover who makes the decisions within the organization.

You must ask value questions.
Discover what is important to them and focus on it.

135

You need doomed spies.
Deceive professionals into being captured.
We let them know our orders.
They then take those orders to our enemy.

You need surviving spies.
Someone must return with a report.

Your job is to build a complete army.
No relations are as intimate as they are with spies.
No rewards are too generous for spies.
No work is as secret as that of spies.

If you aren't clever and wise, you can't use spies.
If you aren't fair and just, you can't use spies.
If you can't see the tiny subtleties, you won't get the truth
from spies.

Pay attention to small, trifling details!
Spies are helpful in every area.

Spies are the first to hear information, so they must not
spread it.
Spies who give your location or talk to others must be killed
along with those to whom they have talked.

You must ask leading questions.
Ask questions that guide customers in a certain direction.
You don't tell them what you want them to believe.
You ask questions that lead them to thinking it themselves.
.
You must ask closing questions.
These are the questions that create the sale.

Your job is to create a good sale.
You can create close customer relationships with questions.
No other skill is as valuable.
No other words should be as carefully prepared.

Questions do not work without the use of common sense.
You must ask only fair and reasonable questions.
You must listen carefully to get any value out of asking questions.

You must pay very careful attention.
You can learn everything from asking the right question.

Questions are the fastest way to get information but you must listen.
Sales people who talk before they have thoroughly listened hurt themselves and their customers.

You may want to attack an army's position.
You may want to attack a certain fortification.
You may want to kill people in a certain place.
You must first know the guarding general.
You must know his left and right flanks.
You must know his hierarchy.
You must know the way in.
You must know where different people are stationed.
We must demand this information from our spies.

I want to know the enemy spies in order to convert new spies
into my men.
You find a source of information and bribe them.
You must bring them in with you.
You must obtain them as double agents and use them as your
emissaries.

Do this correctly and carefully.
You can contact both local and inside spies and obtain their
support.
Do this correctly and carefully.
You create doomed spies by deceiving professionals.
You can use them to give false information.
Do this correctly and carefully.
You must have surviving spies capable of bringing you
information at the right time.

You may want to address a certain market.
You may want to go after a specific business.
You may want to contact a certain decision-maker.
You must first know who the decision-makers are.
You must know their assistants.
You must know their organization.
You must know how to reach them.
You must know who influences their decisions.
You must get this information from your questions.

You must know how to get close to the customer's key people.
You must give them a reason to help you.
You must win them over to your side.
You must ask value questions to learn what is important to them and their company.

You must do this carefully.
You can ask qualifying and identifying questions and learn more.
You must also do this carefully.
You can ask leading questions.
You can use them to guide a person's thinking.
You must do this carefully as well.
You will then know how to ask closing questions at the appropriate time.

These are the five different types of intelligence work.
You must be certain to master them all.
You must be certain to create double agents.
You cannot afford to be too cheap in creating these double
agents.

This technique created the success of ancient emperors.
This is how they held their dynasties.

You must always be careful of your success.
Learn from the past examples.

Be a smart commander and good general.
You do this by using your best and brightest people for
spying.
This is how you achieve the greatest success.
This is how you meet the necessities of war.
The whole army's position and ability to move depends on
these spies.

There are five different types of questions.
You must be certain to master them all.
You must be certain to ask value questions.
You cannot invest too much time understanding customers'
values.

This is the way you make your fortune.
This is how you keep your customers.

You must grow and update your knowledge.
Learn from your past successes and failures.

As a salesperson, you must keep your company informed.
You must use your best ideas and efforts to gather
information.
This is how you make the biggest sales.
This is how you meet your company's needs.
Everything you do depends upon the questions you've
asked.

The *Art of War Plus* Series

Competitor's Guides for Career and Business

Sun Tzu's *The Art of War Plus The Art of Career Building*

$14.95 160 Pages. Paperback, 5 1/2" X 8 1/2". By Gary Gagliardi.
The Art of War plus an adaptation that applies Sun Tzu's lessons to the lifelong process of advancing your professional career. *The Art of War* is shown on the left-hand page; its adaptation as *The Art of Career Building* is on the right-hand page. ISBN: 1929194137.

Sun Tzu's *The Art of War Plus The Art of Starting a Business*

$14.95 160 Pages. Paperback, 5 1/2" X 8 1/2". By Gary Gagliardi.
The Art of War plus an adaptation that applies Sun Tzu's lessons to all the challenges of starting a new business in the modern marketplace. *The Art of War* is shown on the left-hand page; its adaptation as *The Art of Starting a Business* is on the right-hand page. ISBN: 1929194153.

Sun Tzu's *The Art of War Plus The Art of Sales*

$14.95 160 Pages. Paperback, 5 1/2" X 8 1/2". By Gary Gagliardi.
The Art of War plus an adaptation for sales people that applies Sun Tzu's lessons to common sales situations. *The Art of War* is shown on the left-hand page; its adaptation as *The Art of Sales* is on the right-hand page. ISBN: 1929194013.

Sun Tzu's *The Art of War Plus The Art of Management*

$14.95 160 Pages. Paperback, 5 1/2" X 8 1/2". By Gary Gagliardi.
The Art of War plus an adaptation for organization managers that applies Sun Tzu's lessons to managing people, resources, and quality in a modern organization. *The Art of War* is shown on the left-hand page; its adaptation as *The Art of Management* is on the right-hand page. ISBN: 1929194056.

Sun Tzu's *The Art of War Plus The Art of Marketing*

$14.95 160 Pages. Paperback, 5 1/2" X 8 1/2". By Gary Gagliardi.
The Art of War plus an adaptation that applies Sun Tzu's lessons to winning modern marketing warfare. *The Art of War* is shown on the left-hand page; its adaptation as *The Art of Marketing* is on the right-hand page. ISBN: 1929194021.

Competitor's Guides for Mastering Sun Tzu

Sun Tzu's **The Art of War** *Plus* **Sun Tzu's Own Words**

$9.95 160 Pages. Paperback, 5 1/2" X 8 1/2". Translated by Gary Gagliardi. The most accurate translation of the ancient classic. A character by character translation of the Chinese ideograms is on the left-hand page. The corresponding English sentences are on the facing right-hand page. ISBN 1929194005

Sun Tzu's **The Art of War** *Plus* **The Amazing Secrets of Sun Tzu**

$14.95 160 Pages. Paperback, 5 1/2" X 8 1/2". By Gary Gagliardi The best explanation of the hidden elements in the text. The complete text of *The Art of War* on the left-hand page. On the facing right-hand page, the secrets hidden in the text are explained in words and pictures. ISBN 1929194072.

Sun Tzu's **The Art of War** *Plus* **The Warrior Class**

$29.95 320 Pages. Paperback, 5 1/2" X 8 1/2". By Gary Gagliardi An detailed discussion of each stanza of Sun Tzu's *The Art of War*. Each stanza is explained in depth for its use in modern competition. ISBN: 1929194099.

Competitor's Guides for Your Personal Life
(Available Summer, 2002)

Sun Tzu's **The Art of War** *Plus* **The Art of Winning Love**

$14.95 160 Pages. Paperback, 5 1/2" X 8 1/2". By Gary Gagliardi *The Art of War* plus an adaptation for finding, winning, and holding onto a lifelong love. *The Art of War* is shown on the left-hand page; its adaptation as *The Art of Winning Love* is on the right-hand page. ISBN: 1929194145.

Sun Tzu's **The Art of War** *Plus* **The Art of Parenting Teens**

$14.95 160 Pages. Paperback, 5 1/2" X 8 1/2". By Gary Gagliardi *The Art of War* plus an adaptation for keeping your teen alive and well until you can get them safely out of the house. *The Art of War* is shown on the left-hand page; its adaptation as *The Art of Parenting Teenagers* is on the right-hand page. ISBN: 1929194161.

More Competitor's Guides Planned!
Check www.clearbridge.com for the latest information!

Audio and Video

Amazing Secrets of Sun Tzu's The Art of War VIDEO
Plus Amazing Secrets Companion Book
$49.95. 1 1/2 Hours. VHS. 160-Page Book by Gary Gagliardi.
A video recording of a live presentation by Gary Gagliardi on the sophisticated system of competition hidden in Sun Tzu's *The Art of War.* The book, *The Art of War Plus The Amazing Secrets of Sun Tzu,* contains the complete *Art of War* text and a detailed explanation of the seminar topic, ISBN 1929194110. Video without book $39.95, ISBN 1929194080.

Amazing Secrets of Sun Tzu's The Art of War CD SET
Plus Amazing Secrets Companion Book
$39.95. 1 1/2 Hours. Set: Two CDs. 160-Page Book by Gary Gagliardi.
A recording of a live presentation by Gary Gagliardi on the sophisticated system of competition hidden in Sun Tzu The Art of War. The book, *The Art of War Plus The Amazing Secrets of Sun Tzu,* contains the complete *Art of War* text and detailed explanation of the seminar topic. ISBN 1929194129. CD Set without book $29.95, ISBN 1929194102.

Speaking and Training
Gary Gagliardi, the author of **The Art of War *Plus*** series, is available for a *limited* number of speaking engagements. Contact Becky Wilson at Clearbridge Publishing: 206-533-9357.

Volume Discounts
All Clearbridge titles are available at a discount when purchased in quantity. Titles can be combined to qualify for discounts.

Discount Schedule

Total # of Items	Percentage Discount
5-9	15%
10-49	30%
50-99	40%
100-249	45%
250-499	46%
500-990	48%

Fax orders to Clearbridge. FAX: 206-546-9756.

Clearbridge Order Form

Fax 206-546-9756

Company Name:_____

Contact Person:_____

Shipping Address:_____

City State Zip:_____
Phone Number: _____ Fax Number: _____

Quantity	ISBN	Title	Retail	Total Retail
_____	1929194005	AOW & Sun Tzu's Own Words	$9.95	_____
_____	1929194013	AOW & The Art of Sales	$14.95	_____
_____	1929194021	AOW & The Art of Marketing	$14.95	_____
_____	1929194056	AOW & The Art of Management	$14.95	_____
_____	1929194072	AOW & Amazing Secrets of Sun Tzu	$14.95	_____
_____	1929194099	AOW & The Warrior Class	$29.95	_____
_____	1929194137	AOW & The Art of Career Building	$14.95	_____
_____	1929194145	AOW & The Art of Winning Love	$14.95	_____
_____	1929194153	AOW & The Art of Starting a Business	$14.95	_____
_____	1929194161	AOW & The Art of Parenting Teens	$14.95	_____
_____	1929194110	Amazing Secrets Video & Book	$49.95	_____
_____	1929194129	Amazing Secrets CD Set & Book	$39.95	_____

_____Total # Titles   Total Retail: $_____

Less Discount (See previous page.): $_____

Credit Card Information   Total: $_____
(Visa, MasterCard, or   Shipping charges are added to Total.
American Express only.)   Shipping is UPS Ground FOB Seattle.

Name on Card: _____

Card Address:_____

City, State, Zip:_____

Credit Card Number:_____

Expiration Date:_____ Signature:_____

The Warrior Class Training Site
FREE to Clearbridge Book Owners ONLY!
On-line Training in Sun Tzu's Methods

FREE 300-Page E-Book: *The Warrior Class.* In this e-book, each stanza of *The Art of War* is explained in detail. Available on-line in Acrobat format.

FREE Slide Shows: Fourteen free slide shows, one for each chapter of *The Art of War* plus an overview. Over 300 HTML slides.

FREE Self-scoring Tests: Two tests on each chapter, one on the text and one on the concepts in *The Warrior Class* e-book.

PASSWORDS are contained in this book for accessing *The Warrior Class.*

Go to www.clearbridge.com/training-area.htm for the User ID and page number in this book with the current password.